D1255687

SUCCESS

SUCCESS

**Discovering
the Path to Riches**

NAPOLEON HILL

ST. MARTIN'S
ESSENTIALS
NEW YORK

First published in the United States by St. Martin's Essentials, an imprint of St. Martin's Publishing Group

www.stmartins.com

Designed by Steven Seighman

Endpaper pattern © LenLis/Shutterstock.com

The Library of Congress Cataloging-in-Publication Data is available upon request.

ISBN 978-1-250-22054-7 (hardcover)
ISBN 978-1-250-22055-4 (ebook)

Our books may be purchased in bulk for promotional, educational, or business use. Please contact your local bookseller or the Macmillan Corporate and Premium Sales Department at 1-800-221-7945, extension 5442, or by email at MacmillanSpecialMarkets@macmillan.com.

First Edition: November 2019

10 9 8 7 6 5 4 3 2 1

ANYBODY can wish for riches,
and most people do, but only a few know
that a definite plan, plus a burning desire
for wealth, are the only dependable means
of accumulating wealth.

—NAPOLEON HILL

CONTENTS

INTRODUCTION

Napoleon Hill

Most of us are asking for success without the usual hardships that come with it. We want success with as little effort as possible.

I do not know what your definition of the term success is, but if I may impose my own definition on you, I would do so as follows:

Success is the sum total of one's acts and thoughts that have, on account of their positive, constructive nature, brought happiness and good cheer to the majority of those with whom one has been associated in the past and the majority of those with whom one will be thrown in contact in the coming years.

You cannot possibly bring happiness, good cheer, and sunshine into the lives of those with whom you associate and not enjoy success. Neither can you bring misery, despondency, and unhappiness to others and be a success.

If you cause other people to smile when you are near, if you carry with you the rich, vibrating, dynamic personality that causes people to be glad when you are near, if you speak and think of the beauties of life and persuade others to do the same, if you have eliminated cynicism, hatred, fear, and despondency from your own nature and filled their place with a wholesome love for humanity, then you are bound to be a success!

Money is not necessarily evidence of success. It may be, in fact, evidence of failure, and will be, if happiness and goodwill did not accompany it throughout the process through which it was accumulated.

I value more highly than all the material wealth in the world the pleasure—the thrilling joy—that has come to me as the result of the opportunity I have had during the past years to serve my fellow man.

Could any amount of money buy happiness? NO! A thousand times, NO! Pleasure comes from doing and not acquiring. This is a lesson that some people never seem to learn, but it is a truth nevertheless.

The roadway to that thing we call success leads in one direction and that is straight through to the great field of human service. Any other road that leads in another direction cannot lead one to success.

I want to be happier this year than I was last year; not by acquiring more worldly goods, although I could use them to my advantage, but by serving others and by bringing greater happiness to the members of my immediate family and my personal friends.

If we cannot increase our measure of success in this manner, then we know not how to do so!

By no means do I recommend that anyone give up the pursuit of money as one means of finding success and happiness, but I strongly recommend that no one depend entirely upon the power of money for success and wealth.

I never have had enough money to cause me to quit trying to render service, but some who I know have had, and the result is not what I would call success.

Success in life produces wealth, but not the kind many think of; rather it is happiness and peace of mind that is derived by rendering service to others.

—NAPOLEON HILL, 1920

Napoleon Hill

Do you know that there is a big difference between an idle wish for the attainment of a definite object and a burning desire to attain it? Anybody can wish for things, and most people do, but only a few know how to desire so deeply that it turns into a flame of resolute determination.

—NAPOLEON HILL

PREFACE

Don M. Green

If you mention success, the majority of people believe that you are talking only about money. In fact, those individuals with a lot of money are considered by most to be successful people.

This little book on success will explore this aspect of success, which is made up of money and material possessions. However, this book will also focus on other, more important elements of success, such as family, friends, and good health.

When Ralston Society published Napoleon Hill's classic book, *Think and Grow Rich,* in 1937, it was a hardcover book with a paper dust jacket. The original book cover contained the following phrase, "For Men and Women Who Resent Poverty." However, in later publications, that phrase was removed and was replaced with the number of copies sold.

Part of the appeal of *Think and Grow Rich* comes from the title itself. At the time it was written, people across the country were experiencing the Great Depression and were looking for a way to make a living. Readers across the nation read *Think and Grow Rich* and it not only changed their financial situation, but also brought hope to a dismal time period. So, clearly, Napoleon Hill sought to teach his readers how to obtain material success. But he wanted them to obtain other measures of success as well.

Napoleon Hill spent a lifetime studying successful people to understand why some are successful and others are not. His interviews with more than five hundred of the most successful people of his time helped him answer that question. Additionally, Hill interviewed thousands of people he deemed unsuccessful. Hill often stated that he learned more from these unsuccessful individuals than he did from the successful ones.

After these many years of interviews and research, Napoleon Hill discovered that many successful people shared common traits and practiced the same principles. He used these principles to write his first book, *The Law of Success,* in 1928. The first publication of this book was an eight-volume set with each book containing two success principles.

Napoleon Hill called this material in *The Law of Success* a course created for the serious-minded individual who wanted to devote at least a portion of his or her time to learn how to succeed in life. He had two purposes in mind for this: to help students find their weaknesses and to create a plan that would provide the means to correct these weaknesses.

Some of the many weaknesses that inhibit us from being successful are:

- *Greed*
- *Intolerance*
- *Jealousy*
- *Revenge*
- *Egotism*

In order to obtain wealth of any kind, certain steps must be followed by any person. To begin with, a definite chief aim or major purpose must be established. This is a goal that you hope to achieve and it allows you to concentrate your talents and efforts on one task at a time. A definite major purpose also keeps you from wasting time and energy on useless projects. This was the second of the sixteen principles discussed in *The Law of Success,* and was a major focus of the book.

The fifteen other steps to success discussed in *The Law of Success* are listed below and will allow you to achieve any form of wealth you want from life.

The Master Mind Principle is the first one explained in *The Law of Success,* and it is of primary importance. It refers to the harmonious co-operation of two or more people who ally themselves for the purpose of achieving a shared objective. This principle almost miraculously creates a "Master Mind," which is greater than the sum of its parts, that is, it is more powerful and capable than the individual minds that are working in harmony.

Self-Confidence will help you master the six basic fears which everybody faces. These are the fear of poverty, old age, ill health, criticism, loss of love, and death. Self-confidence will teach you the difference between egotism and real self-assurance, the

By and Large, There is No Such Thing as Something for Nothing. In the Long Run, You Get Exactly That for Which You Pay, Whether You Are Buying an Automobile or a Loaf of Bread.

—Napoleon Hill

latter of which is based upon definite skills and knowledge that you can put to use.

The habit of saving will teach you how to distribute your money because part of all that you earn should remain with you. This will allow you to accumulate funds in case of an emergency, or for investing. Learning to pay yourself first is one of the most important steps to achieving financial wealth. It is impossible to have financial success unless you develop the habit of saving.

Personal initiative and leadership are two qualities that must be developed to attain success. It will be much easier to achieve success in any field if you are willing to take the lead in any situation and act with initiative.

Imagination will stimulate your mind so you can receive new ideas and develop plans to help you achieve your definite aim in life.

Enthusiasm is a quality that is the foundation of a pleasing personality, which is a great asset to help you succeed.

Self-Control is an absolute necessity for anyone who desires wealth. This principle corresponds directly with the habit of saving, in that you must control your money if you want to be financially successful. People who do not have self-control end up being controlled by others.

Going the extra mile simply means that you do more than you are paid to do. This is the one thing you can do without permission, but sooner or later, it will help you stand out in a crowd.

A pleasing personality is one quality that makes a good salesperson. We are all selling something, whether it is physical goods or services. Becoming a master salesperson is essential to being wealthy in any field.

Accurate thinking is also beneficial on the road to success.

Concentration is the ability to focus on only one goal or objective at a time. If you desire to be wealthy, you must be able to control your mind and direct it to thoughts that will help you achieve your goal.

Cooperation is another necessary step to achieving success. It is the ability to work with others in a sense of harmony.

Learning from failure is simply being able to learn from your mistakes. It gives you the ability to start over when something goes wrong and to find a different solution for the problem.

Tolerance teaches a person how to avoid the disastrous effects of racial and religious prejudice. Intolerance is a major cause of defeat for millions of people who allow themselves to be entangled in foolish arguments, thereby poisoning their minds and closing the door to reason. It makes enemies of friends, destroys opportunities, and fills the mind with doubt and mistrust.

Practicing the Golden Rule will teach you how to make use of this great universal law of human conduct. It will allow you to get harmonious cooperation from any individual or group of individuals. Lack of understanding the law upon which the Golden Rule philosophy is based is one of the major causes of failure of millions of people who remain in misery and poverty!

Those who don't understand the Golden Rule often argue that it doesn't work. They are inclined to think in terms of "an eye for an eye, and a tooth for a tooth," which is nothing more nor less than the law of retaliation. If they would go a step further in their reasoning, they would realize that

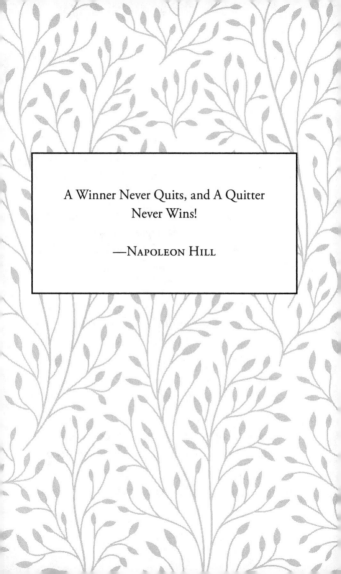

A Winner Never Quits, and A Quitter
Never Wins!

—NAPOLEON HILL

they are only looking at the negative effects of this law.

In the book you are about to read, the Napoleon Hill Foundation has compiled and edited works by Napoleon Hill which demonstrate how these sixteen principles of success I just described can guide you to the wealth you desire and deserve.

The first chapter focuses on how learning to help others can bring you true happiness and mental and emotional wealth. And as Napoleon Hill points out, service to others can also bring you financial wealth while you are helping others.

The next chapter is a brief essay on the necessity of planning if you want to become a leader in your business or personal life. This essay will inspire you to stop being a follower and to become the leader you can be.

Chapter three tells the fascinating story of how Jack London, famous American author of *The Call of the Wild,* and other best-selling novels, used determination and concentration to overcome countless temporary defeats and to attain wealth. His perseverance paid off so greatly that he eventually earned $75,000 per year from his books, a fabulous sum in the early 1900s when he first achieved success and wealth.

The next chapter is devoted to the success principle Napoleon referred to as Controlled Attention. In it he details the achievements of such men as President Woodrow Wilson and inventors Thomas Edison, Elmer Gates, and Alexander Graham Bell, quoting at length from his interviews with them, and explaining how they attained success and greatness through application of this principle.

Chapter Five is derived from one of the Mental Dynamite booklets Napoleon wrote in 1941, just before the entry of the United States into World War II. It explains how success can only be achieved by carefully planning the use of one's time, and then resolutely carrying out the plans. Napoleon shows how this need for budgeting impacts not only monetary wealth but also the wealth of happiness available to all families.

The next chapter stresses the importance of team work in attaining financial wealth in one's business or profession. It also explains the need for team work in achieving the wealth provided by a happy and harmonious family life.

Chapter Seven teaches how application of the Golden Rule benefits not only those who are aided by its practitioner, but also the practitioner himself. Thomas Edison was one of the great examples of the use of this principle, and his story is told here.

The next chapter concentrates on the Power of Attraction. Taken from a never completed treatise on psychology, it explains how a positive or negative mental attitude, interacting with the law of the Power of Attraction, operates either to produce success or to deny it.

Chapter Nine is a brief essay in which Napoleon details how wealth can be used to better the person who has it as well as others who receive the benefit of it through philanthropy. Most of the great men studied by Napoleon Hill in his lifelong search for the principles of success achieved true wealth and peace of mind by acts of philanthropy.

In chapter Ten, Napoleon introduces a brief but brilliant essay by James Allen on the role played by luck in achieving success. You guessed it—it plays no role at all!

The next chapter deals with the role played by Autosuggestion in implanting habits on the subconscious mind. The thoughts impressed on the subconscious then produce their physical counterparts. Here Napoleon explains in detail how to use autosuggestion to obtain wealth.

Chapter Twelve explains the importance of Faith in achieving wealth, and how it interplays with other success principles. Faith as understood by Napoleon was not necessarily religious belief, but rather belief, confidence, conviction, assurance and dedication to a goal, followed by action. The Wright Brothers, Christopher Columbus, and Albert Einstein are featured as examples of how the application of Faith can lead to success.

The final chapter deals with the principle of Self-Discipline. Some consider this to be the master key to success because without it none of the other principles can be effective. Napoleon explains the interrelationship of self-discipline with these other principles.

I hope you will enjoy and benefit from this little book about success, and that it will lead you to all the success you desire.

—DON M. GREEN
Executive Director
Napoleon Hill Foundation

SUCCESS

If You Must Slander Someone,
Don't Speak It, But Write It in the
Sand near the Water's Edge!

—NAPOLEON HILL

The person who is eternally driven by a burning desire for the achievement of some definite objective is practically sure to find ways and means of attaining it.

—NAPOLEON HILL

LEARN TO SERVE OTHERS

The amount of wealth you obtain in life will depend a great deal on the number of people you serve. First, let us be prepared to recognize riches when they come within our reach. Some believe that riches consist in money alone! But, enduring riches in the broader sense consist of many other values than those of material things, and I may add that without those other intangible values the possession of money will not bring the happiness which some believe it will provide.

When I speak of riches, I have in mind the greatest riches whose possessors have made life pay off on their own terms—the terms of full and complete happiness. These riches of life will benefit all those who are prepared to receive them. I am sure most people have heard or read the saying, "When the student is ready the teacher will appear." Are you prepared to receive them?

All riches, of whatever nature, begin as a state of mind which is the one and only thing over which any person has complete, unchallenged right of control.

It is highly significant that the Creator provided man with control over nothing except the power to shape his own thoughts and the privilege of fitting them to any pattern of his choice.

Mental attitude is important because it converts the brain into the equivalent of an electromagnet which attracts the counterparts of one's dominating thoughts, aims, and purposes. It can also attract the counterpart of one's fears, worries, and doubts.

A positive mental attitude, or PMA, as many refer to it, is the starting point of all riches, whether they be riches of a material or intangible nature.

It attracts the riches of true friendship and the riches one finds in the hope of future achievement.

It provides the riches one may find in nature's handiwork, as it exists in the moonlit nights, the

This is an age when service is uppermost in the minds of men. The person who finds a better way of rendering even the most humble sort of service may write his own salary ticket and collect it without protest. If you can improve the wrapper on a package of goods, or dress a window more attractively, or find a way to create greater harmony among the people who work with you, you are on the great highway to sure success, if you put your ability into action.

—NAPOLEON HILL

stars that float in the heavens, beautiful landscapes, and distant horizons.

It supplies the motivation and inspires the mind to find the means to assist others.

PMA also gives one the riches found in the labor of one's choice, where expression may be given to the highest reaches of man's soul. It also gives the riches of harmony in relationships, where all members work together in a spirit of friendly cooperation.

Lastly, a positive mental attitude provides the riches of sound mental health, which is a treasure to those who have learned the importance of maintaining good physical health.

Every adversity has within it the seed of an equal or greater benefit. The story of Milo Jones is an excellent example of overcoming adversity and attaining wealth by serving others.

Milo Jones was a farmer when he became paralyzed and learned he would never walk again. While he was confined to his bed, he had plenty of time to think about how to overcome his situation and provide for his family. As a result, he decided that he would use his farm to raise pigs, which in

One reason why the person who performs more service and better service than he is paid for is always in demand is the fact that he meets with little competition in this practice.

—NAPOLEON HILL

When riches begin to come, they come
so quickly, in such great abundance, that
one wonders where they have been hiding
during all those lean years.

—Napoleon Hill

There are no limitations to the mind
except those we acknowledge.

—Napoleon Hill

If you form the habit of rendering more service and better service than that for which you are paid, very soon the Law of Increasing Returns will begin to work in your favor.

—NAPOLEON HILL

turn, would be used to produce sausages to sell. His little idea quickly allowed him to become one of the largest breakfast sausage manufacturers in the country. Even in his terrible condition, Milo used his mind to think and plan. He learned a lesson on how to serve others and became wealthy in the process.

It is a human tendency to obtain more of the best things life has to offer because it is human nature to want more from life. Many of us seek the economic security that money can provide. And, by truly serving others, we can receive money in exchange for our efforts to serve others. Remember, there is no such thing as something for nothing.

The sure way to lasting wealth is by providing excellent service to others. However, many people set their definite major purpose on money first, and service second. This is not the way it should be. You should set your mind on the clear idea of helping others in any way you can, and money will follow.

The habit of working with a definite chief aim will help you develop the habit of making prompt decisions, and this outstanding habit will help you in all that you do in life. Having a definite chief aim in mind will help you concentrate your efforts on the task at hand.

A definite chief aim and concentration are two traits that always go hand-in-hand. These traits will always be found in highly successful people and each trait assists the other.

The most successful men and women are those who make prompt decisions and only focus on one definite chief aim at a time. For instance, F. W. Woolworth had one task in mind when he set out to build the largest chain of Five and Ten Cent stores. William Wrigley, Jr. had the sole idea of selling chewing gum until he made his fortune. Edwin C. Barnes concentrated on his definite chief aim, becoming Thomas Edison's partner, and he became Edison's only business partner. Likewise, Abraham Lincoln, Henry Ford, Andrew Carnegie, George Eastman, and thousands of other individuals have succeeded on their own terms because they knew how to focus and concentrate their efforts.

There are also many examples of people who focus only on mistakes and adversity. These people concentrate on poverty, failure, discouragement,

It is a peculiar trait of human nature, but it is true, that the most successful men will work harder for the sake of rendering useful service than they will for money alone.

—NAPOLEON HILL

The worst day in a man's life is when he sits down and begins thinking how he can get something for nothing.

—THOMAS JEFFERSON

unhappiness, and other negative thoughts, and nature provides their physical equivalent.

It only takes one idea of performing a better service or creating a better product that will lead you on your way to success and wealth. If you make this your definite chief aim and concentrate all your efforts on this task, you will reach a level of success that most people only dream about.

In *Think and Grow Rich,* I wrote, "In every chapter, mention has been made of the money-making secret that has made fortunes for more than 500 exceedingly wealthy men whom I have carefully analyzed over a period of many years. The secret was brought to my attention by Andrew Carnegie more than a quarter of a century ago. The secret to which I refer has been mentioned no fewer than 100 times throughout this book. It has not been directly named for it seems to work more successfully when it is merely uncovered and left in sight, where those who are ready and searching for it may pick it up. That is why Mr. Carnegie tossed it to me so quietly, without giving me its specific name.

If you are ready to put it to use, you will recognize the secret at least once in every chapter. I wish

I could tell you how you will know when you are ready to receive the secret, but that would deprive you of much of the benefit you will receive when you make the discovery in your own way.

There is no such thing as something for nothing. The secret to which I refer cannot be had without a price, although the price is far less than its value. It cannot be had at any price by those who are not intentionally searching for it. It cannot be given away. It cannot be purchased for money, for the reason it comes in two parts. One part is already in possession of those who are ready for it."

Are you prepared to learn the secret? Service to others will surely help prepare you.

PLANNING THE SALE
OF SERVICES

Learning the ways and means of marketing personal services is important for any of those who wish to sell their services in the marketplace. It is even more important for those people who aspire to leadership roles, in whatever career or field they may be engaged.

Intelligent planning is necessary for success in any venture, and the same is true for the accumulation of riches.

There are only two real ways of making a living, and they are by selling products or selling services. If you are in a service field, it should inspire you that most of the great fortunes that have been accumulated started from the sale of services or an idea.

There are two types of people in the world; one

is known as the leader and the other is known as the follower. Early in your career, you should decide which of these people you would like to be. Leaders are paid higher wages than followers and followers will be disappointed if they expect to earn the same as a leader.

I would like to point out that there is nothing wrong with being a follower. But, that doesn't mean you have to be a follower your whole life. Most leaders started out as good followers and progressed.

It is important to realize the traits that are necessary for those of you who wish to be in a leadership position. First you will need courage and the ability to take responsibility for your choices or actions, and then you will need self-control because the person who can't control himself won't be able to lead others.

A good leader must be able to make quick decisions and a good leader must plan his work and work his plan. Going the extra mile is another trait leaders must possess.

There are two forms of leadership of which you should be aware. The most effective form of leadership is leadership by consent, which means the followers agree with you as a leader. The other form of leadership is leadership by force, where you do not possess the consent and sympathy of the followers. History shows us that leadership by force cannot last.

We are all salespeople. I have taught many thousands of people how to sell and, believe me, it takes planning and deciding how to lead yourself and your "customers" to take the path you want to wealth. Plan your work, then work your sales plan, and you will be on your way to wealth.

Useful ideas are generally the creation of people who make it their business to render more service and better service than that for which they are paid; they are seldom created by those who do just enough with which to "get by."

—NAPOLEON HILL

If you wait until you are entirely ready, until you have in hand everything that you need for success, you will never get anywhere because worthwhile success is something that can be achieved only by the person who starts where he stands, and has the imagination and courage to meet emergencies as they arise. If you wait until the time is right for you to begin, you might as well give up hope, for the time will never be just right. Do the best you can with the tools at hand; other and better tools will become available when necessity becomes greater.

—NAPOLEON HILL

THE MAN WHO DARED TO FAIL

Did you ever hear of a man gambling security against an unproved dream and winning $75,000 a year?

Jack London did. He became the leading literary figure of his day in America, and attained a yearly income of $75,000 because he dared to gamble security against an untried longing in his heart.

There were dozens of reasons why Jack London could not become a writer–good, substantial reasons that everybody saw except Jack himself. He attended high school for only one year. The associations of his youth had been not among people who knew anything of literature, but among oyster pirates and the crews of tramp steamers. There was a wild, untamed quality in his spirit that had made him a sailor familiar with every port of the world before he was sixteen. It was an unquenchable lust for red-blooded adventure that seemed to be so at odds with the conventional quietness of the literary life.

Against this he could place nothing except a love for reading and the determination to become a writer—a determination that came to him while his ship was off the shores of Japan.

It hardly had docked in San Francisco before he wrote to the University of California to request its entrance requirements. He learned that he would have to pass an entrance examination before he could enter—an examination on the knowledge he would have gained from high school.

Undaunted, he filled his room with high school textbooks, and laid out a study plan. During the day, he worked at whatever job he could get: newsboy, janitor, laundry worker, furnace stoker. At night, propped up in bed, he studied. He put a set of wooden spikes under his pillow, so that they struck him when he dozed off, and forced him upright again.

For a full summer he labored like this, and in

Temporary defeat does not mean failure. Great leaders accept defeat only as a signal for greater effort.

—Napoleon Hill

the fall he took the entrance examinations and passed.

But he did not find the things he sought in the university. The academic approach to knowledge was deadly to his untrammeled spirit. At the end of the first semester, he quit college, bitter and disappointed.

But he continued his killing pace of self education, working by day, writing by night.

He took a civil service examination for rural mail carrier and passed. The call came. His name was first on the list, and he was given one day in which to accept. All through a weary night, he sat in bed thinking deeply. If he accepted the job, he had the promise of security for the rest of his life. His mother and sisters were wild for him to take it. This was his first chance at steady work with a guaranteed decent wage.

On the other hand, to accept meant to yield up his writing, to sacrifice his dream, to spike for all time his grim determination. It meant the end of his burning desire to give to the world what he had seen of the stark, the red-blooded, the tragic.

At last he fell into weary sleep. He awoke and

looked about the room. He saw the piles of books, the reams of manuscripts, the battered typewriter. One look in the clear light of morning was enough.

He reported to the Post Office Department, asked for deferment, and was told to take the post immediately or forget it forever.

"I'll forget it," he said, and walked out—back to a weary, soul-sickening grind of work at anything by day, and long, eye-burning, heart-shrinking writing by night.

The manuscripts went out in a never-ending stream, and flowed back to his desk, rejected. He pawned his bicycle, his books, his clothing—everything except his typewriter.

Then one morning, as he counted the returned manuscripts which the postman had left, a letter fell from between two of the large envelopes. He ripped it open and unfolded the single sheet with trembling hands.

The Saturday Evening Post offered him $750 for the first American serial rights to *The Call of the Wild,* and shortly thereafter he sold the book rights to another publisher for $2,000.

The long days of hunger and doubt were over. In a few years the dream had come astoundingly true. Jack London was earning $75,000 a year.

This story of phenomenal success clearly illustrates the first principle of success—definiteness of purpose. Jack London the tramp-steamer sailor became Jack London the writer because a fire was kindled in his heart and he determined to become a writer. Without that determination, that burning desire, we can easily imagine him dying in a knife fight in Singapore.

That principle of definiteness of purpose is behind all success, and London's story graphically illustrates it. Perhaps the biggest decision he ever made in his life, after that night off the shore of Japan when he determined to write, was the choice of his dream against the security of a government position.

Jack London gambled that night with tremendous stakes! He dared to fail for his belief—and he held to his definite purpose. Concentration and determination produced for him the wealth he dreamed of.

In the past many years I have analyzed 25,000

men and women in America. Ninety-eight percent of them are failures. And every failure has lacked a definite purpose in life. The two percent who succeeded, without exception, have had a definite major aim in life, coupled with a burning desire to achieve it, and for them success and wealth have followed as the night follows the day!

CONTROLLED ATTENTION

Let us give attention to a feature of controlled attention which suggests the way to wealth, through a combination of principles. It is often found to produce success when combined with four other success principles I have studied.

We know from observation and experience that the following principles, when assembled in the mind through a combination of thoughts, may produce mind power bordering upon the "miraculous":

(a) Definiteness of Purpose
(b) Self-Discipline, through control of the emotions
(c) Controlled Attention

(d) Imagination, applied to the object of one's purpose

(e) Applied Faith, actively engaged

Here is a combination of principles capable of helping to solve almost any problem by which one is confronted. The power comes from the combination, not from any single principle. Let us see how the principles are applied to produce mind power which leads to success and wealth:

Let us say that a man is faced by one of the commonest of all problems, the need of a certain amount of money for some specific purpose. There are two major ways of dealing with the problem. First, he can fret about it but do nothing to raise the money. This is the usual way of handling such problems. Or, he can tackle it head-on BY COMBINING THE FIVE PRINCIPLES HERE MENTIONED AND GOING AFTER THE MONEY IN EARNEST.

Here is how to apply the five principles:

The amount of money required is known and one has made up his mind to get it. That is Definiteness of Purpose.

The mind is cleared of all fear and doubt that

the money cannot be procured. That is Self-Discipline.

The mind is put to work acquiring the money, to the exclusion of all other problems. That is Controlled Attention.

The mind is put to work through the faculty of the Imagination on creating something of an equivalent value that is to be given in return for the money.

The mind is given repeated suggestions that the amount of money desired will be procured, no matter what the cost may be or what conditions have to be complied with. That is Applied Faith, in action,

When these five principles are combined, and applied in the manner described, the subconscious mind goes to work and creates a plan by which the money may be procured.

THE COMBINATION OF THE FIVE PRINCIPLES I HAVE MENTIONED PROVIDES ONE WITH POWER THAT IS NOT ATTRIBUTABLE TO ANY ONE OF THESE PRINCIPLES ALONE. The experiences of men of great achievement bear this out. First I will refer you to the great inventor, Thomas A. Edison, whose statement to me on the subject is quoted as nearly verbatim as memory will permit:

"You ask me," said Mr. Edison, "to name the most important characteristics of a successful inventor. Well, I can describe them very briefly. They consist, first, of definite knowledge as to what one wants to achieve. (Definiteness of Purpose.) One must fix his mind on that purpose with that sort of persistence which knows no such word as 'impossible,' making use of all the accumulated knowledge on the subject he can find, and drawing upon experience. (Controlled Attention, Imagination) He must keep on searching, no matter how many times his search is unsuccessful. (Applied Faith) He must refuse to be influenced by the fact that someone else may have tried the same idea without success. (Self-discipline) He must remain convinced that the solution of his problem exists somewhere, and that he will find it." (Applied Faith)

Then Mr. Edison said, "When a man makes up his mind to solve a problem he may, at first, meet with opposition; but if he persists and keeps searching he will be sure to find the solution. I never knew

Education means development from within. The word "educate" comes from the Latin word *educo,* which means "to induce, to draw out, to develop from the inside." Instruction is not education, because instruction does not always cause the human brain to develop from within.

—Napoleon Hill

the plan to fail." (A combination of all five of the principles is involved here.)

"The trouble with most people," he continued, "is that they never really act. They quit before they start." By this he meant, of course, that self-imposed limitations prohibit most people from beginning tasks which they might easily complete if they made a start and kept on going.

"In all my work," Mr. Edison said, "I never found the solution to any problem connected with an invention through my first efforts, with the exception of the talking machine. And one of the most surprising of all things is that when I have finally discovered that for which I was searching, I generally found that the answer was within my reach all the time, but nothing but persistence and a will to win would have uncovered it."

Dr. Alexander Graham Bell, the inventor of the modern telephone, explained his invention in the following terms:

"I discovered the principle of the long-distance telephone while searching for the means of producing a mechanical hearing aid for the benefit of my wife, whose hearing was impaired. I made up my mind to find that hearing device if it required the remainder of my life. After many failures I finally uncovered the principle for which I was searching, and was astounded at its simplicity. I was even more astounded to discover that the principle I revealed was not only beneficial in the construction of a mechanical hearing aid, but it served also as a means of sending the sound of the voice over a wire."

DR. BELL MADE USE OF ALL FIVE OF THE PRINCIPLES HERE DESCRIBED, ALTHOUGH HE MAY HAVE DONE SO UNCONSCIOUSLY. "Another discovery that grew out of my work," said Dr. Bell, "was the fact that when a man gives his brain an order to produce a definite result, it seems to have the effect of giving him a 'second sight' that enables him to see right through ordinary problems. What this power is I do not know; all I know is that it exists, and it becomes available only when a man is in that state of mind in which he knows exactly what he wants and is determined to get just that."

John Wanamaker, the late "merchant king of Philadelphia" used CONTROLLED ATTENTION and these other principles to solve business problems. He told the following story about dealing with one such problem:

"On numerous occasions during the early part of my business career," said Mr. Wanamaker, "I found myself in need of funds which I could not obtain through any of the usual commercial or banking channels. On every such occasion I made it my practice to go to the park and begin walking, thinking as I walked of new approaches to the solution of my problem. Once I needed a very large sum, because we had a slow selling season and found our shelves stocked with merchandise we could not sell. I made up my mind not to go back to the store until I had solved my problem. I kept my mind on it and at the end of the second hour an idea came to me that enabled me to walk right back to the store and raise the necessary amount of money within fifteen minutes. The strangest part of the experience was that I did not think of that idea at the start."

CONTROLLED ATTENTION, PLUS DEFINITENESS OF PURPOSE, FORMED THE

COMBINATION THAT SERVED MR. WANA-MAKER IN THIS INSTANCE. Perhaps Applied Faith and Imagination were a part of the combination of principles he used, but of these principles he made no mention. He did say, however, that "I doubt that there is any such reality as an unsolvable problem for the man who has learned how to apply his mind with a firm determination to find its solution." That was the equivalent to saying that there is no such thing as an unsolvable problem for the man who knows how to use imagination and faith.

Dr. Elmer R. Gates, a scientist and inventor of three decades ago, once explained to me how he used the principle of Controlled Attention:

"There is some hidden source of power," said Dr. Gates, "which comes to a man's aid when he sets his mind on a definite goal and becomes determined to attain it. That is how I have uncovered the secrets of more than 200 inventions, not one of which existed in my knowledge at the beginning of my search. I can fix my attention on a problem and keep it fixed until the solution of the problem seems to float into my mind from the air. The greatest difficulty is that of maintaining sufficient willpower to keep my mind concentrated upon a single purpose long enough to let me tap this mysterious source of inward sight."

Let us have a word now from the late President Woodrow Wilson, whom I had the privilege to advise:

"When the written request came from the German military authorities for an armistice, in 1918," said Mr. Wilson, "it presented one of the greatest problems of my Presidency. I knew a decision had to be made and that the lives of thousands of people depended upon that decision. I laid the paper aside for a few minutes, closed my eyes, and determined to seek guidance from a source greater than my own faculty of reason. In a little while I picked up the paper and walked onto the porch of the White House, stood there with my eyes closed, the paper clenched in my hand, and asked for Divine guidance. In a little while the answer came! It was so obviously sound, that I went right back to my study and wrote the reply to the Germans in shorthand. Subsequent events proved that I made

Intellectual, organized thought is the beginning of all constructive achievement.

—NAPOLEON HILL

the right decision, for it was but a short time later that the German Kaiser had been dethroned and was on his way into exile."

WHAT WAS THIS STRANGE POWER ON WHICH THE WAR PRESIDENT RELIED FOR HIS ANSWER? HE MADE NO ATTEMPT TO EXPLAIN IT! One can only surmise as to what he believed it to be, but there is one fact of which there is no doubt; he forced his mind with faith and imagination behind it to seek the solution of a grave problem and it produced the desired results. HIS EXPERIENCE WAS CONTROLLED ATTENTION OF THE MOST PROFOUND NATURE.

The purpose of CONTROLLED ATTENTION, as far as this philosophy is concerned, is that of enabling one to bring together all the departments of the mind and harness their combined power for use in connection with a given purpose. THAT IS WHAT CONTROLLED ATTENTION AMOUNTS TO. It often operates with other success principles to bring about the desired result.

The man who has a Definite Major Purpose in life and a definite plan for achieving that purpose has already gone nine-tenths of the distance toward success.

—Napoleon Hill

BUDGETING TIME

Procrastination robs you of opportunity. It is a significant fact that no great leader was ever known to procrastinate in achieving greatness.

You are fortunate if AMBITION drives you into action, never permitting you to falter or turn back, once you have rendered a DECISION to go forward.

Second by second, as the clock ticks off the distance, TIME is running a race with YOU!

Delay means defeat, because no man may ever make up a second of lost TIME.

TIME is a master worker which heals the wounds of failure and disappointment and rights all wrongs and turns all mistakes into capital, but it favors only those who kill off procrastination and remain in ACTION when decisions are to be made.

Life is a great checkerboard. The player opposite you is time.

If you hesitate you will be wiped off the board.

You may be shocked if you keep accurate account of the TIME you waste in a single day.

TIME AND HUMAN RELATIONSHIPS ARE THE TWO MOST IMPORTANT REALITIES OF LIFE!

Both must be properly organized and utilized by the man who succeeds. The man who organizes his time efficiently and relates himself to others harmoniously can have anything he desires, provided only that he knows exactly what he desires and is determined to get it.

There is something about the uncertainty of time that is awe-inspiring, for time is one thing that cannot be bought and it cannot be prolonged by the mere desire to live. However, time is the one thing which most people dissipate carelessly. They spend it in idleness, or in useless effort, as if it were perpetual, whereas, as the life-insurance salesman has so aptly said, one has only a second of time at any given moment of which he can be sure of life.

The late Dr. Elmer R. Gates was so conscious of

the value of his time that he devised a plan to work while he slept, by giving orders to his subconscious mind just before going to sleep. His plan was so successful that he was often awakened during his sleep period by the action of his subconscious mind in presenting to him the solution to some problem he had given it to solve.

Dr. Gates said that he got the idea of inducing his subconscious mind to work while he slept from his experience in using it as an alarm clock to awaken him at any desired minute. He reasoned that if his subconscious faculty could be influenced to attend to so trivial a matter as that of awakening him at a given minute it could also be induced to attend to more important matters, and his reasoning proved to be sound.

USE OF "SPARE TME." Spare time may be defined as that portion of one's time that is not required for one's occupational pursuit, and is available to be devoted to other interests, such as recreation and pleasure, or preparation and planning. The use one makes of his spare time is an accurate source of analysis through which his future may be foretold. The more successful people have found that their greatest opportunity consists in the freedom of thought they employ during their spare time, for it is during this period that one may cultivate the habit of meditation and communion with that secret power from within.

Spare time can be self-promotion time for the person who works for others, for it is during this period of freedom that one may prepare himself for greater responsibilities, through study.

Andrew Carnegie said that he never received a promotion, while he was working for wages, that he could not trace directly to the use he made of his spare time, by doing something he was not paid to do. Each of the five hundred or more distinguished men who aided in organizing this philosophy said substantially the same thing.

The habit of drifting is a costly habit, however it is indulged, but "costly" is hardly the word to describe it when one drifts in the use of his spare time. "Tragedy" would be a more descriptive word, for the neglect of one's free time is nothing short of tragedy.

If one must be a waster of any portion of his time he would be wiser to waste a part of his sleep

There is always plenty of capital for legitimate purpose, but no man with a "poverty consciousness" can get a cent of it for any purpose. Capital has a peculiar way of getting into the hands of those who are successful and who carry the atmosphere of success with them wherever they go.

—NAPOLEON HILL

period than to waste, by neglect or dissipation, his spare time, for as paradoxical as it may seem, a man's spare time should be his busiest time.

The drifter wastes time as if it were something to be endured instead of a priceless asset to be used wisely. The waste grows out of the fact that THE MAJORITY OF PEOPLE HAVE NO SUCH THING AS A BUDGET SYSTEM BY WHICH THEY USE THEIR TIME, due to the fact they drift from day to day without definiteness on any subject.

Wasted time is one of the greatest of all sins human beings commit against themselves. O. Henry discovered this fact after he had been sentenced to prison for embezzlement. While sitting in his prison cell it occurred to him that his imprisonment was no handicap, but an advantage of priceless value. It gave him an opportunity, the first he had ever enjoyed, in fact, to use his mind any way he chose! He began to use time for the writing of short stories, not only writing his way out of prison, but leaving behind him literature that insured his name a place of respect for centuries to come. Almost overnight O. Henry transformed himself into one of the most respected literary men of his era, by his constructive use of time!

A prominent psychologist once said, "Let me know every thought you think for one day and I will tell you exactly what sort of life you have before you." If you are drifting in your use of time, you are destined to go through life as a failure, unless you turn about-face and organize yourself under a strict schedule through which you will control and direct to a definite end every portion of time as it comes to you.

The family relationship is the most important of all human relationships, for its success requires harmony, understanding, sympathy, and cooperation. The head of the family cannot succeed in his chosen work unless he has the peace of mind that grows out of harmony in his home. Harmony is the result of careful planning, budgeting of income and outgo, and the budgeting of time of every member of the family.

WHEN A MAN AND HIS WIFE WORK TOGETHER HARMONIOUSLY, WITH A DEFINITE GOAL AS THEIR COMMON AIM, THEY ARE SURE TO FIND THE SOLUTION

TO THE PROBLEMS WITH WHICH THEY MEET, NO MATTER HOW SERIOUS THOSE PROBLEMS MAY BE.

The great American way of life has its major source in the American homes, for it is here that the voting power that supports the government exists; it is here that the American wealth is produced and consumed; it is here that the character of the American people is developed; it is here that religion has its roots; it is here that education has its foundation; and let us not forget that it is here that the burden of sickness, misery, poverty, and disappointments of every nature must be borne!

AMERICANISM, IN ALL ITS CONNOTATIONS, IS BUT THE SUM TOTAL OF THE RELATIONSHIPS IN THE AMERICAN HOMES!

Remember this and you will understand why the home relationship is the most important of all human relationships. You will understand, too, why your home should be organized and managed according to a definite plan that has been shaped to produce harmony and cooperation.

Clearly it is the duty of every man to set his own

If you have no major purpose in life, you are licked before you start, no matter how much schooling you may have had.

—NAPOLEON HILL

household straight, and if he refuses or neglects to do so, he cannot hope to enjoy the peace of mind that is necessary for his personal success. Harmony should begin at home. Cooperation should begin at home. Personal initiative should begin at home. Enthusiasm and interest in life should begin at home. Sympathy and understanding should begin at home.

DRIFTING IN IMPORTANT FAMILY RELATIONSHIPS LEADS TO THE DIVORCE COURTS, RESULTS IN POVERTY AND WANT, AND DISTURBS THE PEACE OF MIND OF EVERY MEMBER OF THE FAMILY.

Every family member should have a duty to perform for the good of the group, and the family should be managed as any well-managed business corporation is conducted, with definiteness of purpose, cooperation, harmony, loyalty, and oneness of purpose. The family council should be as regular and as definite in its purpose as a board of directors' meeting in a business firm.

The time that is wasted by men and women who work for salaries and wages is sufficient, in the aggregate, to provide the means of building another industrial system twice the size of the American system of industry. It is sufficient, also, to provide every worker with an additional income as great or greater than that which he now receives for the sort of service he is rendering.

The ways in which workers waste time are too numerous for a complete listing, but here are a few of them:

First of all, they waste time by the wrong sort of mental attitude toward themselves, toward one another, and toward their employers. Much of this negative mental attitude is the result of their wanting something for nothing; wanting more wages and less work; or wanting better jobs without a willingness to prepare themselves to hold them, or the willingness to assume the full responsibilities that go with better jobs.

They waste time by rendering a poor quality of work, due to their negative mental attitude.

They waste time by rendering an inadequate amount of service. Instead of Going the Extra Mile, they neglect to go the mile for which they are paid.

They waste time by unnecessary friction among themselves, caused by petty jealousies.

IF YOU WORK FOR WAGES, YOU SHOULD EXAMINE YOURSELF CLOSELY TO MAKE SURE THAT YOU MAINTAIN A POSITIVE MENTAL ATTITUDE WHILE YOU WORK. And insofar as the conditions of your work will permit, you should make sure that you follow the habit of Going the Extra Mile, in both the quality and the quantity of work you do. And remember that the number of hours you put into your job is no criterion by which to judge your value. The value of your services depends entirely upon the quality and the quantity of work you perform, plus the mental attitude you maintain while you work, and to the extent that you control these you will be in a position to set your own wages and choose your own job.

Budgeting time is essential to the achievement of success, whether measured in money, happiness, or harmony. We have all heard it said that "time is money," and my studies have shown this to be true. Wasted time results in success denied.

TEAMWORK

Success or failure often depends upon the sort of relationships one has with others, because power of sufficient proportions to enable one to attain outstanding success and wealth can be acquired only by the coordination of efforts of one's self and others. I call this coordination TEAMWORK.

Of all the places where teamwork pays the highest dividends, the home comes first. And the benefits go not only to those who occupy the homes, but to the nation as well, for A SUCCESSFUL NATION IS NOTHING BUT A LARGE ASSEMBLY OF HOMES IN WHICH THERE IS SUCCESSFUL HOME LIFE.

Teamwork in the home must begin with the parents, in their relationship with each other. The spirit of friendly cooperation should be taught to the children by the example set by the parents.

The benefits of friendly teamwork between the members of a family are too numerous for detailed mention here, but those of major importance are peace of mind, self-reliance, and the inspiration necessary to influence each member of the family to make some substantial contribution to the family welfare.

The best managed families are those whose individual members are self-disciplined to assume their share of the responsibilities and to do it in a spirit of friendly cooperation. CHILDREN CAN BE DISCIPLINED BY FORCE BUT THEY CANNOT BE MADE TO ENJOY IT, a fact which is well known to any adult who remembers childhood days. And harsh discipline, by force, is known to have ruined more children than it has ever benefitted.

Happy, successful families enjoy an esprit de corps that reflects itself in the personality of every member of the family. This family spirit of friendly cooperation is manifested generously during the one period of the day when all members of the family assemble together, during the meal hour. HERE THEY TAKE FOOD FOR THEIR SPIR-ITUAL WELL-BEING AS WELL AS FOOD FOR THEIR PHYSICAL BODIES.

This is (or should be) the family sacred hour of friendly discussion when all members of the family, from the parents on down to the baby in the highchair, should be permitted to mix love and joy with the food they eat. The food digests more quickly and the character of the children develops positive traits that will benefit them all through life when meals are a pleasant experience.

The minds of children are plastic, flexible and highly receptive to all forms of stimuli, and especially to those inspired by their parents! EVERY WORD SPOKE IN THE PRESENCE OF A CHILD BY ITS PARENTS MAKES A PERMA-NENT RECORD IN THE CHILD'S MIND. Even the facial expression and the tone of voice of the parents become a definite influence upon the child, an influence that remains with it all through life.

It is a common error of parents to assume that the children they bear belong to them, and they have the right to treat them as they would any other chattel, or to punish them at will, by any means they choose. Children do not belong to their parents. The parents are but temporary custodians, at most, who are charged with the responsibility of teaching their offspring, by example as well as by precept, the fundamentals of sound character. Children do not ask to be brought into the world. Their parents are solely responsible.

PARENTS OWE THEIR CHILDREN EVERYTHING THEY CAN GIVE THEM THAT WILL PREPARE THEM TO LIVE THEIR LIVES IN PEACE AND CONTENT- MENT, including, in particular, a good education.

In all human relationships there is one quality which tends to make them permanent and harmonious. It might be summed up in one phrase: RE- SPECT FOR THE RIGHTS OF OTHERS. OR, IT MIGHT BE STATED IN ONE WORD— UNSELFISHNESS!

No form of human relationship can result in permanent teamwork unless all parties to the team contribute wholeheartedly and unselfishly to its maintenance.

Remember that a real leader assumes full responsibility, not only for his own acts, but also for the acts of his subordinates.

—NAPOLEON HILL

This principle applies no less to a family circle than to a business organization where, obviously, exploitation, cheating, dishonesty, or selfishness lead to failure.

Teamwork in the family, to be of the greatest benefit to all members of the family, must be carried on in a spirit of true sportsmanship, without the attempt of any member of the family to dominate any other member by force or coercion! No member of the family should fear another member, and above all, there should be no fear or mistrust upon the part of either of the parents.

No human relationship born of fear and force can long endure, nor can it be fruitful of anything but resentment, hatred, and rebellion upon the part of those who are thus restrained.

Domination of one person by another, through fear and force, is not in harmony with the Creator's plans, proof of which is the fact that EVERY HUMAN BEING WANTS FREEDOM AND LIBERTY ABOVE ANYTHING ELSE EXCEPT THE PRIVILEGE OF LIVING.

The Creator provided every human being with the greatest of all powers with which one may dominate another without resentment or injury. It is the only safe method of domination, and it is the only method that can be relied upon to build permanent human relationships.

It is known as LOVE, the greatest of the human emotions, and it has many forms of application.

Its highest form is that which is expressed in love between a man and a woman; the highest because this form of love (if it is true love and not merely physical attraction) is the nearest approach to the Divine love existing between the Creator and those who are in harmony with Him.

Then, there is the love which exists between parents and their children, provided it has not been infiltrated with fear and force, or weakened by neglect and selfishness.

There is also the love called friendship which binds, in a spirit of harmony and understanding, those who relate themselves unselfishly in any form of teamwork.

The average man's vocation consumes six out of every seven days of his time; therefore the better portion of his life goes into it. That which one gets from his vocation depends upon what he puts into it, with particular emphasis upon three things,

(1) the quality of service rendered, (2) the quantity of service rendered, and (3) the mental attitude in which the service is rendered.

Only by careful attention to these three factors may one be sure of getting the fullest measure of cooperation from those with whom one works. Education, experience, and personal skill will count for nothing if one neglects or refuses to observe and properly apply these three requirements of teamwork.

Now let us analyze the subject of mental attitude and see what constitutes the type which inspires teamwork. Broadly speaking, there are three types of mental attitude: First, the positive type. Next is the neutral, or indifferent type, as expressed by the "drifter" who has no definite major purpose and no particular ambition in life. This type neither offends nor pleases because he just drifts through life.

Then there is the negative type, represented by the person who is out of step with everyone, including himself, and devotes most of his time to thinking about the things he does not want and criticizing the people he does not like. It is needless to say that this type never engages in harmonious

Many a man limits himself and makes promotion impossible because he lacks the courage to teach someone else how to hold down his job. Consequently, when the job higher up is open, he will not get it because his employer has no one to take his place.

—Napoleon Hill

teamwork, and of course he never succeeds at anything because others refuse to cooperate with him.

Harmony, based upon friendly cooperation, gives one power that can be acquired in no other way, and HARMONY BEGINS WITH A POSITIVE MENTAL ATTITUDE ON THE PART OF THE INDIVIDUAL WHO SEEKS THE COOPERATION OF OTHERS.

Individuals everywhere are involved in team relationships in the home, church, school, club, business, community, city, county, state, army, navy, professional society, fraternity, and the nation as a whole, and those who neglect or refuse to be governed by the spirit of friendly teamwork never benefit by the American way of life except by the stray crumbs of circumstance they can snatch here and there.

The "isolationist"—the individual who sets himself up as a part of a small minority in any cause, and refuses to cooperate with the majority in carrying out a harmonious way of life—finds himself hopelessly outmoded and unpopular, and his personal influence reduced to a low minimum.

Where conflict exists in human relationships the

cause may be traced to some form of greed, selfishness, or ignorance, none of which is a part of Nature's laws. Adaptation to Nature's laws leads always to success while failure to adapt leads as definitely to failure, which leaves me no alternative but to conclude that THE WISE MAN IS THE ONE WHO THROWS HIMSELF UPON THE SIDE OF NATURE'S PLANS AND RELATES HIMSELF TO OTHERS IN HARMONY WITH THOSE PLANS.

It was this sort of wisdom, based upon adaptation to natural laws, which produced the geniuses of all ages, through whom the sciences and the more useful of Nature's principles have been unfolded to the world. Thus did Copernicus in astronomy, Columbus in navigation, Plato in philosophy, Edison in invention, Beethoven in music, Michelangelo in art, Marconi in wireless communication, and the Wright Brothers in aeronautics make use of the minds of others in revealing to the world the results of their discoveries.

Teamwork is essential if one wants to be a success in any respect, be it monetary, family happiness, or achievement in society.

THE GOLDEN RULE

The Golden Rule has been recognized and applied by every person who has attained true greatness. It has been recognized by every great religious leader and every true philosopher.

The man of Galilee discovered it and clothed it in the most understandable terms in which it has ever been expressed, in the Sermon on the Mount, when He said, "Therefore all things whatsoever ye would that men should do to you, do ye even so to them."

Many sermons have been preached on the Golden Rule, but few of them have interpreted the full depths of its meaning, the gist of which is this: LOSE YOURSELF IN UNSELFISH SERVICE TO OTHERS AND THEREBY DISCOVER THE MASTER KEY TO THAT POWER

FROM WITHIN WHICH GUIDES ONE, UNERRINGLY, TO THE ATTAINMENT OF ONE'S NOBLEST AIMS AND PURPOSES.

Let us turn, now, to an analysis of the lives of men and women who have applied the Golden Rule so we may observe the spirit and manner in which they related themselves to others.

I shall begin with Andrew Carnegie, who is responsible for development of the Science of Success. At the outset of his career, he adopted the spirit of humility of heart, and this he maintained throughout his life. In his upward climb from poverty to riches, he made it a part of his responsibility to inspire others to share his success, a privilege that extended to the humblest workman in his employ.

Andrew Carnegie thought not in terms of his own welfare alone, but of the welfare of generations yet unborn. He knew the value of the Golden Rule because he had disciplined himself by living by it! The space he occupied, therefore, is as great as the world, and though he has become a citizen of the universe his spirit goes marching on, inspiring men and women through higher education and the reading of books to acquire an understanding of the means to personal success and happiness.

In 1929 Thomas A. Edison enjoyed a celebration of success unparalleled in the history of the world—one which, by contrast, makes the pageants of Roman triumph appear small. The world that contributed to the Roman triumph was a restricted area of only a minor fraction of the earth, but the world that acclaimed Edison for his inventions embraced all the nations of the earth.

No such recognition of individual genius had ever before been witnessed, for this was the first Golden Jubilee in which the world celebrated a triumph of peace, where no prisoners in chains followed the procession of the victor; where malice, envy, and hatred were replaced by universal gratitude for the benefits conferred upon humanity by the one man whose genius had made the sun shine at night through the conversion of its stored energy into a miniature reproduction of its incandescent mass.

"On the twenty-first day of October, in this Jubilee year," said Alfred O. Tate, Edison's former secretary, "the spreading rays of golden light which flooded the country were focused on Dearborn, Michigan, where Henry Ford had organized a celebration in honor of Edison, distinguished not only by its magnificence but also by the ingenuity which reproduced some of the salient events in the history of his career that literally made them live again.

"At seven o'clock in the evening of this day, in the pillared chambers of a replica of Independence Hall in Philadelphia, the most notable gathering of men distinguished in all walks of American life ever assembled under one roof had been convened as the banquet guests to honor Edison.

"The address honoring Edison was delivered by the President of the United States. When Edison arose to reply, he was overcome with emotion which was felt by his whole audience, and he was nearly speechless. It was the first time he had ever attempted to speak in his own behalf at an occasion of this nature. He never again made a similar appearance."

HERE WAS HUMILITY OF THE HEART IN ITS HIGHEST FORM OF MANIFESTATION! AND HERE WAS EVIDENCE THAT

You can have no greater asset than the confidence men place in you. Build on it and add to it. Do not knock the pins out from under it by welshing or repudiating your word. When you agree to do a thing, do it, not because you must, but for the better reason that this will add to the value of your reputation and build new confidence.

—NAPOLEON HILL

THE MAN WHO LOSES HIMSELF IN SER-
VICE FOR THE BENEFIT OF OTHERS WILL
BE DISCOVERED AND ADEQUATELY RE-
WARDED BY THE ACCLAIM OF THOSE
WHO KNOW HIM.

Edison seldom spoke to anyone of his achievements! His motto was "Deeds, not words." He told
me once that talking about himself was a complete
waste of time.

He so lost himself in his work that he had neither
the time nor the inclination to think of himself, and
he has admitted that NEVER, IN HIS ENTIRE
LIFE, DID HE GIVE SERIOUS THOUGHT AS
TO WHAT HE MIGHT GET FOR HIS LABOR.
HIS GREATEST CONCERN WAS IN CON-
NECTION WITH WHAT HE MIGHT GIVE!
His entire life was a gift to others, with not a thought
given to what he would receive in return.

The world has been talking about the Golden
Rule for nearly 2,000 years, and thousands of
sermons have been preached about it, but ONLY
A FEW HAVE DISCOVERED THAT ITS
POWER CONSISTS IN ITS APPLICATION,

NOT MERELY IN THE BELIEF OF ITS SOUNDNESS.

Now I wish to explain some of the major benefits of the Golden Rule.

Because motive is of major importance in all human relationships, let us take inventory of the benefits one may receive by applying the Golden Rule, and determine how many of the basic motives one acts upon in applying this rule of human conduct, viz.:

1. The motive of LOVE: This, the greatest of all the emotions, is founded on the Golden Rule spirit which inspires one to put aside selfishness, greed, and envy, and relate himself to others as if he were in their place. The motive of love, expressed through the Golden Rule philosophy, enables one to comply freely with that age-old admonition to "Love they neighbor as thyself." It brings one to a full recognition of the oneness of mankind, through which it becomes obvious that ANYTHING WHICH DAMAGES

ONE'S NEIGHBORS DAMAGES ALSO HIMSELF. Let us, therefore, apply the Golden Rule in all human relationships as a practical means of demonstrating the spirit of true brotherhood. This is the greatest of all motives for applying this profound rule.

2. The PROFIT MOTIVE: This is a sound and universal motive, but too often it is expressed in a selfish spirit. Financial gains attained through application of the Golden Rule, however, are more enduring. They carry with them the goodwill of those from whom the gains are attained. This sort of gain establishes no ill will or animosity, no envy toward the one who gains it. It carries with it a form of willing cooperation from others that can be had in no other way.

3. The motive of SELF-PRESERVATION: The desire for self-preservation is inborn in all of us. This goal can best be attained by those who, in their efforts to reach it, aid others in their attainment of the same desire. The rule of "Live and let live," when applied, insures a like response from

others. THUS THE GOLDEN RULE BE-COMES THE SUREST METHOD OF ATTAINING SELF-PRESERVATION, THROUGH THE FRIENDLY COOP-ERATION OF OTHERS.

4. The motive of desire for FREEDOM OF BODY AND MIND: There can be no free-dom of either body or mind for the person whose neighbors do not have similar freedom. There is a common bond which affects all people, and just dues are meted out to the man who tries to take more than his fair share of the gains, or to dodge his share of the losses. THE MAN WHO GAINS FREEDOM OF BODY AND MIND MORE QUICKLY IS THE MAN WHO AIDS OTHERS IN ATTAINING SIMI-LAR FREEDOM. Freedom must become the common property of one's neighbors and associates if it is to be enjoyed by one's self.

5. The motive of desire for POWER AND FAME: Fame is something a man may ac-quire only by the consent of others. It is something existing outside of one's own

If you wish to know what is fair and just in your dealings with your fellow men, reverse every situation that you are about to create for the other fellow and see yourself in his place. If you would not be delighted to take the part which you have laid out for the other fellow, you may be sure the transaction is not based upon justice.

—NAPOLEON HILL

mind. Therefore it is outside of one's control except by the leave of others. Power, too, is something that can be attained only through the cooperation of others. Thus, BOTH POWER AND FAME, THE DESIRE FOR WHICH IS ONE OF THE BASIC MOTIVES OF MANKIND, ARE CIRCUMSTANCES THAT CAN BE ATTAINED ONLY THROUGH THE FRIENDLY COOPERATION OF OTHERS, THROUGH THE APPLICATION OF THE GOLDEN RULE.

One may profit by the slogan of the Rotary Clubs, "He profits most who serves best." One cannot "serve best" without putting himself in the place of those he serves, in every form of relationship. One cannot acquire and hold power and fame without benefitting others in proportion to the benefits he himself enjoys. This is why ONE SHOULD PRACTICE AS WELL AS PREACH THE SOUNDNESS OF THE GOLDEN RULE! IT IS THE PRACTICE THAT YIELDS DIVIDENDS, NOT MERELY THE BELIEF IN THE RULE.

An educated person is one who knows how
to get everything he wants without violating
the rights of other people.

—NAPOLEON HILL

THE POWER OF ATTRACTION

The great negative note in the lives of most people is Fear. Fear is the mother of all the negative emotions, and her brood is found clustering very closely around her. Worry, Lack of Confidence, Bashfulness, Irresolution, Timidity, Depression, and all the rest of the negative family of feelings and emotions are the progeny of Fear. Without Fear none of these minor emotions or feelings would exist. By killing off the parent of this brood of mental vampires, you escape the coming generations of negative thoughts, and thus keep your Mental Attitude gardens free from these pests and nuisances.

Fear and the emotions that come from it do more to paralyze useful effort, good work, and finely thought-out plans than anything else known to man. It is the great hobgoblin of the race. It has ruined the lives of thousands of people. It has destroyed the finely budding characters of men and women, and made negative individuals of them in the place of strong, reliant, courageous doers of useful things.

Worry is the oldest child of Fear. It settles down upon one's mind, and crowds out all of the developing good things to be found there. Like the cuckoo in the sparrow's nest, it destroys the rightful occupants of the mind. Laid there as an egg by its parent, Fear, Worry soon hatches out and begins to make trouble. In place of the cheerful and positive "I Can and I Will" harmony, Worry begins to rasp out in raucous tones: "Supposin," "What if," "But," "I can't," "I'm unlucky," "I never could do things right," "Things never turn out right with me," and so on until all the minor notes have been sounded. It makes one sick bodily and inert mentally. It retards one's progress, and is a constant stumbling block in one's path upward.

The worst thing about Fear and Worry is that while they exhaust a great deal of the energy of the average person, they give nothing in return. Nobody ever accomplished a single thing by reason of Fear and Worry. Fear and Worry never helped one along a single inch on the road to success and wealth. And they never will, because their whole tendency is to retard progress, not advance it. The majority of things that we fear and worry about never come to pass at all, and the few that do actually materialize are never as bad as we feared they would be. It is not the cares, trials, and troubles of today that unnerve us and break us down—it is the troubles that we fear may come some time in the future. We usually find the way to bear the burdens of tomorrow, the next day, and the day after that, when they arrive. The worry is worse than the reality.

The energy, work, activity, and thought that we expend on these imaginary "maybe" troubles of the future if redirected would enable us to master and conquer the troubles of each day as they arise. Nature gives each of us a reserve supply of strength and energy upon which to draw and to oppose unexpected trouble and problems as they come upon us each day. But we poor, silly mortals draw upon this reserve force and dissipate it in combating the imaginary troubles of next week, or next year, the majority of which never really put in an appearance. When we have need of the force to oppose some real trouble of the day we find ourselves bankrupt of power and energy, and are apt to go down in defeat, or else be compelled to beat an inglorious retreat.

I tell you, friends, that if you once learn the secret of killing off this vampire of Fear, and thus prevent the rearing of her hateful brood of troublesome emotions, life will seem a different thing to you. You will begin to realize what it is to live. You will learn what it is to have a mind cleared of weeds and free to grow healthy thoughts, feelings, emotions, and ambitions.

You will find out that with Fear defeated, you will cease to give out to others the suggestions of incompetence, lack of reliance on yourself, and the other impressions that hurt one's chances. You will find that when you are rid of Fear you will radiate hope, and confidence, and ability, and will impress all those with whom you come in contact.

You will find also that eradication of Fear will work wonders for your Mental Attitude, and for

The only lasting favor which the parent may confer upon the child is that of helping the child to help itself.

—NAPOLEON HILL

the operation of it through the Law of Attraction. When one fears a thing he really attracts it to him, just as if he desired it. The reason is this—when one desires or fears a thing (in either case the principle is the same) he creates a mental picture of the thing, which mental picture has a tendency toward materialization. With this mental picture in his mind—if he holds to it long enough—he draws the things or conditions to him, and thus "thought takes form in action and being." Fortunately, the majority of our fears and worries are silly little things that take possession of our thoughts for a moment and then are gone. They are great wasters of energy, but we do not concentrate on any one of them long enough to put into operation the Law of Attraction.

So you see that unless you get rid of Fear, it will tend to draw toward you the thing you fear, or else force you toward the thing itself. Fear makes of the feared object a flame around which you circle and flutter, like the moth, until at last you make a plunge right into the heat of the flame and are consumed. Defeat Fear, by all means.

But, "how may I defeat it?" you cry. Very easily! This is the method: Suppose you had a roomful of darkness. Would you start to shovel or sweep out the darkness? Or would you not throw open the windows and admit the light? When the light pours in, the darkness disappears. So it is with the darkness of Fear—throw open the windows, and "let a little sunshine in." Let the thoughts, feelings, and ideals of Courage, Confidence, and Fearlessness pour into your mind, and Fear will vanish. Whenever Fear shows itself in your mind, administer the antidote of Fearlessness immediately. Say to yourself: 'I am Fearless; I Fear Nothing; I am Courageous.' Let the sunshine pour in.

You remember the saying of the sacred writer: 'As a man thinketh in his heart, so is he.' A truer statement never was uttered. For every man or woman is what he or she is by reason of what he or she has thought. We have thought ourselves into what we are. One's place in life is largely determined by his Mental Attitude.

Mental Attitude is the sum of one's thoughts, ideas, ideals, feelings, and beliefs. You are constantly at work building up a Mental Attitude, which is not only making your character but which is also having its influence upon the outside world, both in the direction of your effect upon other people, as well as your quality of attracting toward yourself that which is in harmony with the prevailing mental state held by you. Is it not most important, then, that this building should be done with the best possible materials—according to the best plan—with the best tools?

The keynote of this chapter is: "A Positive Mental Attitude Wins Success." Before going any further, let me define the word "Positive" and its opposite, "Negative," and then see how the former wins success and the latter attracts failure. In the sense in which I use the terms, "Positive" means Confident Expectation, Self-Confidence, Courage, Initiative, Energy, Optimism, Expectation of Good, not Evil—of Wealth, not Poverty—Belief in Oneself; "Negative" means Fear, Worry, Expectation of Undesirable Things, Lack of Confidence in Oneself.

Positive Mental Attitude tends toward success by its power in the direction of "making us over" into individuals possessing qualities conducive to success. Many people go through the world bemoaning their lack of the faculties, qualities, or temperament that they instinctively recognize are active factors in the attainment of success. They see others who possess these desirable qualities moving steadily forward to their goal, and they also feel if they themselves were but possessed of these same qualities they, too, might attain the same desirable results.

So far, their reasoning is all right—but they do not go far enough. They fail here because they imagine that since they have not the desired qualities at the moment, they can never expect to possess them. They regard their minds as something that once fixed and built can never be improved upon, repaired, rebuilt, or enlarged. Right here is where the majority of people "fall down," to use the expressive although slangy words of the day.

As a matter of fact, the great scientific authorities of the present time distinctly teach that man, by diligent care and practice, may completely change his character, temperament, and habits. He may eliminate undesirable traits of character, and replace them with new and desirable traits, qualities, and faculties. The brain is now known to be but the instrument and tool of something called the mind, which uses the brain as its instrument of expression.

Let us consider another phase of the impact of Mental Attitude on success. I allude to the effect upon others of one's Mental Attitude. Did you ever stop long enough to think that we are constantly giving other people suggestive impressions of ourselves and our qualities? Do you not know that, if you go about with the Mental Attitude of Discouragement, Fear, Lack of Self-Confidence, and all the other negative qualities of mind, other people are sure to catch the impression and govern themselves toward you accordingly?

Let a man come into your presence for the purpose of doing business with you and if he lacks confidence in himself and in the things he wishes to sell you, you will at once catch his spirit and will feel that you have no confidence in him or the things he is offering. You will catch his mental atmosphere at once, and he will suffer thereby. But let this same man fill himself up with thoughts, feelings, and ideals of Enthusiasm, Success, Self-Confidence and Confidence in his proposition, and he will fairly radiate success toward you. You will unconsciously "take stock" in him and interest in his goods, and the chances are that you will be willing and glad to do business with him.

Do you not know men who radiate Failure, Discouragement, and "I can't"? Are you not affected by their manifested Mental Attitude to their detriment? On the other hand, do you not know men who are filled with Confidence, Courage, Enthusiasm, Fearlessness, and Energy, so that the moment you come into their presence, or they into yours, you at once catch their spirit, and respond thereto? I contend that there is an actual atmosphere surrounding each of these men—which if you are sensitive enough you can feel—one of repulsion, and the other of attraction. These atmospheres are the result of the constant daily thought of these men or the Mental Attitude of each toward life. Think over this a bit, and you will see at once just how the law works.

Yet another example of the impact of Mental Attitude on success may be called the working of the Law of Attraction. All thinking, observing men have noticed the operation of a mental Law of Attraction, whereby "like attracts like."

A man's Mental Attitude acts as a magnet, attracting to him the things, objects, circumstances, environments, and people in harmony with that Mental Attitude. If we think of success firmly and hold it properly before us, it tends to build up a constant Mental Attitude which invariably attracts to us the things conducive to its attainment and materialization. If we emphasize the ideal of Financial Success—in short, Money—our Mental Attitude will gradually form and crystallize the money ideal. And the things pertaining to Money—people calculated to help us win Money—circumstances tending to bring us Money—opportunities for making Money—will be attracted toward us.

You think this is visionary talk, do you? Well, then, just make a careful study of any man who has attained financial success and see whether or not his prevailing attitude is not that of expectation of money. He holds this Mental Attitude as an ideal, and he is constantly realizing that ideal.

Fix your mind firmly upon anything, good or bad, in the world, and you attract it to you or are attracted to it in obedience to the law of attraction. You attract to you the things you expect. Think

You are a human magnet and you are constantly attracting to you people whose character harmonizes with your own.

—Napoleon Hill

about and hold it in your mind. This is no superstitious idea, but a firmly established, scientific fact.

To further illustrate the workings of the above law, that "like attracts like," and "birds of a feather flock together," I might here present the theory which of late has been the subject of much discussion among noted scholars, i.e., that there are thought currents in the mental realm, just as there are air currents in the atmosphere, and ocean currents in the seas. For instance, there are thought currents of vice and others of virtue; thought currents of fear and others of courage; thought currents of hate and others of love; thought currents of poverty and others of wealth. Further than this, the person who thinks and talks and expects poverty is drawn into poverty through currents of the world and attracts to himself others who think and talk along the same lines; and vice versa: the person who thinks, talks, and expects wealth and prosperity attracts, or is attracted to, people of wealth and comes, in time, to share their prosperity with them.

I am not trying to champion this theory, but if it should be true it behooves each one of us to watch our thought and talk, getting rid of the poverty thought, and in its place substituting the wealth and prosperity thought.

Sweep out from the chambers of your mind all these miserable negative thoughts like "I can't," "That's just my luck," "I knew I'd fail," "Poor me," and then fill up the mind with the positive, invigorating, helpful, forceful compelling ideals of success, confidence, and expectation of that which you desire. Just as the steel filings fly to the attraction of the magnet, so will that which you need fly to you in response to this great natural principle of mental action—the Law of Attraction. Begin this very moment and build up a new ideal—that of Success—see it mentally—expect it—demand it!

Remember, your only real limitation is the one that you set up in your own mind.

—Napoleon Hill

Neither a borrower, nor a lender be;
For loan oft loses both itself and friend,
And borrowing dulls the edge of husbandry.
This above all; to thine own self be true,
And it must follow, as the night the day,
Thou canst not then be false to any man.

—William Shakespeare

Your reputation is what people believe you to be; your character is what you really are. Build your character strongly, and your reputation can look out for itself.

—NAPOLEON HILL

PEACE OF MIND

There are several uses for money. The primary use of money is to provide us with our basic necessities, such as food, shelter, and clothing. This use of money applies to every person in the world, young or old, rich or poor. But life should be more than just having our needs met, and that is where the other uses of money become important.

The second use of money is to aid us in times of emergencies, such as illness or loss of income. At some point in life, as well, most people reach a point where they are not physically able to work anymore.

The third use of money enables a person to live the so-called "good life." This includes being able to travel, visit a restaurant, or buy products without worrying about having sufficient funds. In other words, once our basic needs are met and we have set aside money for a rainy day, we can use money to enjoy all that life has to offer.

Lastly, the fourth use of money is to give to or help those in need. Once you reach the stage in life in which you have all the money you will likely ever need, you can start helping individuals or charities of your choosing. Maybe your desire to help will be in providing young adults the chance to receive a college education, or by giving to your church. Maybe you will want to help your community or make a donation that funds medical research.

In life, we choose to be part of the solution or part of the problem. We can either hoard our money while the world suffers, or use what we have been given to enrich the lives of others. The choice is entirely up to us.

You can if you think you can.

—Napoleon Hill

Both poverty and riches are the offspring of thought.

—NAPOLEON HILL

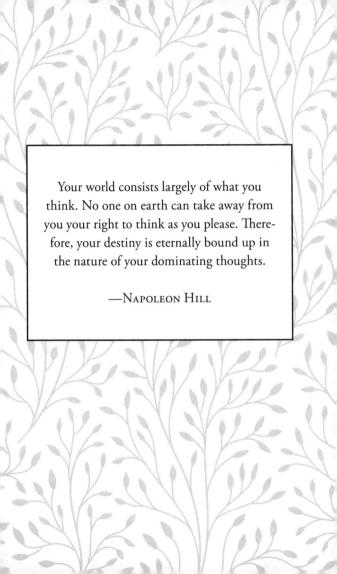

Your world consists largely of what you think. No one on earth can take away from you your right to think as you please. Therefore, your destiny is eternally bound up in the nature of your dominating thoughts.

—Napoleon Hill

Your dominating thoughts have a tendency
to externalize themselves. If you wish to
change your financial status, first change
your dominating thoughts.

—Napoleon Hill

LUCK

So many who have failed to attain wealth look upon those who have as being blessed by good luck. How wrong they are! Vision and effort, not luck, produce wealth, as James Allen has taught us in the following essay:

The thoughtless, ignorant, and indolent, seeing only the apparent effects of things and not the things themselves, talk of luck, of fortune, and of chance. Seeing a man grow rich, they say, "how lucky he is!" Observing another become intellectual, they exclaim, "how highly favored is he!" And noting the saintly character and wide influence of another they remark, "how chance favors him at every turn!" They do not see the trials, failures, and struggles which these men have encountered in order to gain their experiences, and have no knowledge of the sacrifices they have made, of the undaunted efforts they have put forth, of the faith they have exercised that they may overcome the apparently unsurmountable and realize the vision of their heart. They do not know the darkness and the heartaches. They only see the light and joy and call it "luck"; they do not see the long arduous journey, but only behold the achieved goal, and call it "good fortune." These people do not understand the process, but only perceive the result and call it "chance."

In all human affairs, there are efforts and there are results. The strength of the effort is the measure of the result. Gifts, powers, and material, intellectual, and spiritual possessions are the fruits of effort. They are thoughts completed, objects accomplished, and visions realized.

The vision that you glorify in your mind, the ideal that you enthrone in your heart—this you will build your life by, this you will become.

—James Allen

The greatest achievement was at first, and for a time, just a dream. The oak sleeps in the acorn; the bird waits in the egg, and in the highest visions of the soul, a waking angel stirs. Dreams are the seedlings of realities!

—James Allen

AUTOSUGGESTION

Autosuggestion is the medium for influencing the subconscious mind and it impacts everything we see, taste, smell, hear, or touch. It may help to think of autosuggestion as self-suggestion or communicating between your conscious and subconscious mind.

The principle of autosuggestion simply means that our dominating thoughts reach our subconscious mind and influence our actions, and it doesn't matter if these thoughts are positive or negative—they will reach our subconscious mind and then we will see the physical equivalent.

All of the stimuli that we absorb through our senses are first stopped by our conscious mind, because this is where we make a deliberate effort to accept or reject whatever is being placed in front of us. The conscious mind can be thought of as a shield or protection for the subconscious mind, because it has the ability to control what enters our subconscious mind, yet, most of us fail to exert this control, which is why most people are not truly successful.

The subconscious mind has been compared to a rich garden spot. The soil is fertile and full of nutrients and it will readily produce the fruit of whatever seed is planted. You know from your own experience that we all have the power to choose what seeds or suggestions we plant in our subconscious mind. We can plant suggestions that bring forth positive results, or negative ones that lead us in the opposite direction of success.

So, you are probably wondering, how does autosuggestion work? One of the biggest ways of implanting an idea or thought in your subconscious mind is by repetition. We all learn better once we practice and repeat any subject, which is evident in how we learn mathematics or arithmetic: practice, practice, practice—repeat, repeat, repeat. The best way to plant your definite major purpose in your subconscious is by writing your goals down and re-reading that list at least twice daily. You need to be able to see yourself in possession of what you have written down, if you hope to achieve it.

By clearly writing and defining your goals, you are communicating what you desire most to your subconscious mind, and then repetition creates thought habits which will assist you in transforming your goals into their physical counterpart.

Any thought that is regularly repeated will become permanent in your mind. In primary school you learned your times tables and years later, if someone asks you what eight times eight is, you can recall this information with ease. The same is true for any goals, thoughts, or habits that you impress upon the subconscious mind.

However, and this is important, instructions must be given to the subconscious mind with passion and emotion to be effective. The subconscious mind only acts upon those thoughts that are delivered with faith and emotions. The failure to use emotions and the failure to properly apply faith are two of the reasons that autosuggestion does not bring about desired results in most people's lives.

It will require time and patience in order to control and direct your emotions. However, remember, there is no such thing as something for nothing. The ability to reach and influence your subconscious mind has its price, and you should expect to pay that price and the price of ability to influence your subconscious mind is everlasting persistence in the application of the principle. You should not expect to develop the ability for a lower price. Nobody but you can determine if the reward you are striving for is worth the price you must pay for it using your own efforts.

The principle of autosuggestion does not depend on the law of averages and plays no favorites. It will work for all people, regardless of their place in life. When failure is experienced, it is not the principle of autosuggestion that should be blamed; the principle worked and the fault lies with the person. When you do fail, keep trying, make another effort, and another, until you succeed, and you will realize that nothing can replace persistence on the journey to success.

Your ability to use the power of autosuggestion will largely depend upon your ability to concentrate upon a given desire until that desire becomes a burning obsession. Study the principle of concentration and you will learn the importance of focusing your efforts on one definite goal until it is burned into your subconscious, and then habit takes over.

The subconscious mind takes any order that is given to it in a spirit of absolute faith and acts upon this order. Repetition of your thoughts will further impress this order on your subconscious mind. If the goal has not been attained, it is important to constantly repeat this order to your subconscious mind until the goal is obtained.

Remember, too, that the subconscious mind will accept negative as well as positive thoughts—it makes no distinction and imposes no judgment. So it is a blessing to the positive thinker, but a detriment to those who are fearful and negative.

The thoughts that are planted in your subconscious mind will always become their physical counterparts. Imagination can help you attain your goal and is very beneficial in creating plans that will lead you to the attainment of your definite major purpose.

One should not wait until a definite plan, including all steps needed to attain it, has been established

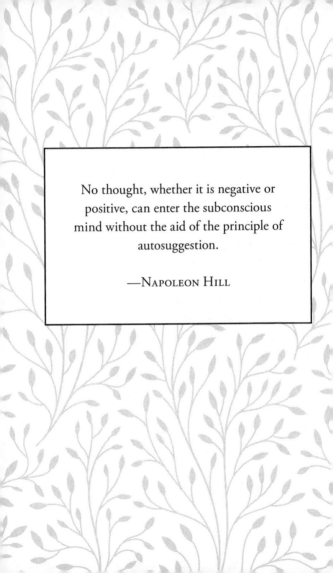

No thought, whether it is negative or positive, can enter the subconscious mind without the aid of the principle of autosuggestion.

—NAPOLEON HILL

in order to begin the journey to success. For instance, if you're desiring financial wealth, you shouldn't wait until you have all of the steps in place or wait for the perfect time to begin. There will never be a perfect time, so you must begin at once to see yourself in possession of that wealth.

When you see yourself in possession of the money, trust that your subconscious mind will provide the right plans at the right time and be on the alert for these plans, for you never know when they will appear, and when they do appear, act immediately! When the plans for obtaining your definite major purpose appear, it is likely that they will "flash" into your mind, in the form of an idea. This idea, inspiration, or message is a direct telegram from Infinite Intelligence. Respect the message and take action at once as failure to do so may well be fatal to your success.

While visualizing the wealth you intend to accumulate, you must also see yourself rendering the service or delivering the product that will give you this money. This is very important and, it is worth repeating—you can never obtain something for nothing.

Ideas are the beginning of all successful achievement. Nothing is as productive of useful ideas as the exchange of thoughts between groups of people who are earnestly interested in each other's welfare. A man would seldom go wrong in his decisions and business plans if he had the privilege of counseling with half a dozen men who would offer him constructive analysis of his plans.

—NAPOLEON HILL

SUMMARY OF AUTOSUGGESTION AND WHAT IT CAN MEAN FOR YOU

Studying my success principles with humility will lead you to obtain greater results in your lives. You cannot follow some instructions, while ignoring others, and hope to succeed. Moreover, it is not enough to merely read all of the instructions that are presented here. You must also take action backed by faith in the belief that you can obtain the desires you are seeking.

The first step in developing a definite major purpose for your life is to go to a quiet place where you won't be disturbed and with your eyes closed, practice "seeing" what you desire most and repeat out loud the desire you want. This is beneficial because when you can hear your goal it will be implanted in your subconscious mind. Next, write down a statement of exactly what you want to obtain. If you are seeking money, be sure to include the exact amount of money you want and a time frame for obtaining it. Also, be sure to clearly write what you want to give up in exchange for this money. When you carry out these instructions, you will quickly be on the path to success.

An example of this would be that you hope to have $20,000 by the first day in January, five years from now. You will have to sell a product or service that will allow you to get this money. Perhaps you could work as an accountant, lawyer, or doctor. Perhaps you will become a salesperson. Whatever your goal may be, you must give something in order to reach it. You can never expect to get something without providing something equivalent in return. Your personal goal statement may look something like this:

By the first day of January, I will have in my possession $20,000. In return for this money, I will give the most efficient service of which I am capable, rendering the fullest possible quantity and the best possibly quality of service in the capacity of salesman of real estate.

I believe that I will have this money in my possession. My faith is so strong that I can now see this money before my eyes, I can touch it with my hands. It is awaiting transfer to me at this time, and is in direct proportion to the service I intend to render for it. I am awaiting a plan to accumulate this money, and I will follow this plan when it is received.

Repeat your personal goal statement out loud every night and every morning, until you are in possession of your definite major purpose. Just don't do this where strangers can hear you, or they will think you have lost your mind.

The purpose of autosuggestion is to place thoughts and ideas into your subconscious mind. Your subconscious mind will only act on those thoughts that are emotionalized by you and given to the subconscious with a "feeling" of faith. Of course, the stronger your emotions and faith are, the more likely your goal will be accomplished.

These instructions, especially in the beginning, may seem to be only a thought or an idea, but don't let that concern you. Follow the instructions, no matter how little you understand them, or how impractical they may seem to be. Sooner or later, if you follow the instructions with persistence, faith, and action, the power of the universe will open up to you.

If you are skeptical about a new idea, you are not in the minority. But remember that all change, whether for an individual or a nation, comes from one idea and sometimes these ideas are viewed as strange, impractical, or unattainable until the results are seen.

Philosophers have often made the statement that man is the master of his own destiny, but most haven't mentioned why this is so. The biggest reason why man is the master of himself and his environment is because he has the power to influence his own subconscious mind and, through it, gain the cooperation of Infinite Intelligence.

The following poem illustrates very beautifully and dramatically the tremendous power of autosuggestion and the role of faith and persistence in reaching our goals:

Invictus
William Ernest Henley

Out of the night that covers me,

Black as the pit from pole to
      pole,

I thank whatever the gods may
      be,

For my unconquerable
      soul.

In the fell clutch of circum-
      stance

I have not winced nor cried
      aloud.

Under the bludgeonings of
      chance,

My head is bloody, but un-
bowed.

Beyond this place of wrath and
tears

Looms but the Horror of the
shade,

And yet the menace of the years

Finds, and shall find, me un-
afraid.

It matters not how strait the
gate,

How charged with punishments
the scroll,

I am the master of my fate.

I am the captain of my soul.

Through the law of harmonious attraction, "troubles" are generally found where they are welcome; they go where they have been invited.

—NAPOLEON HILL

If The Thing You Wish To Do Is Right, and You Believe In It, Go Ahead and Do It! Put Your Dream Across, and Never Mind What "They" Say If You Meet With Temporary Defeat, For They, Perhaps, Do Not Know that EVERY FAILURE BRINGS WITH IT THE SEED OF AN EQUIVALENT BENEFIT.

—Napoleon Hill

Success Requires No Apologies; Failure Permits No Alibis.

—Napoleon Hill

FAITH

The greatest of all miracles is faith, and miracles are happening each and every day.

By looking at history, we realize that miracles happened that forever changed the course of humanity and have benefited mankind all over the world. Edison gave us the lightbulb after thousands of ideas that didn't work out. He also gave us the phonograph, which allowed the human voice to be recorded and reproduced, and which has allowed us to enjoy lectures and music in the comfort of our own homes. These miracles were possible because Thomas Edison possessed faith and the belief that he could accomplish his goals no matter what obstacles stood in his way. No other force may have guided him as strongly as the faith he had in himself.

Most of the pessimistic, unhappy, and fearful things we believe, caused by negative thinking, such as our belief in our own limitations, are simply not true. Many of us believe that there are no more opportunities available in this century; all of the inventions, products, and worthwhile ideas have been used up. However, that is not true and we can find evidence of this in *Acres of Diamonds* by Russell Conwell. The story's message is that we don't have to search wide and far for opportunities. Instead, we can find an abundance of opportunities in the very place where we are if we just have faith.

If we possess adequate faith, opportunity can be found anywhere. The idea that the grass will be greener on the other side is usually false and will lead to constantly and fruitlessly searching for more and better things. Believe me, this is a sure way to never reach success, to fail over and over again.

The Wright Brothers possessed faith that they could accomplish something that had never been done before. They spent many years of trial and error and attempted many dangerous experiments before their airplane conquered the air. Their simple acts of faith that the impossible could become possible changed the world, brought people closer together and made it possible to transport goods and people at a pace that the world had not even dreamed of. Society would never be the same, and this wouldn't have happened if the Wright Brothers didn't have faith in their abilities. As a young reporter, I witnessed their first successful flight, an experience I will never forget.

When Christopher Columbus began his journey seeking passage to the New World, he acted upon an idea and faith. The route Columbus was searching for had never been found, yet he believed that he would be the one to find it, and it required an enormous amount of faith to take those three little ships—the NINA, the PINTA, and the SANTA MARIA—across the Atlantic Ocean, which, of course, was a long and dangerous trip, and sometimes still is. It took strong faith to be able to see the end result, even before the ships set sail.

If you study the history of India, you will quickly realize that Mahatma Gandhi used faith in his beliefs and goals and the belief in himself to combine the forces of 200 million people and break the power of the world's largest army, without firing a shot. The British Empire had ruled India for nearly 200 years, and at its height was the largest empire in history. However, Gandhi proved that faith, backed by action, can bring drastic change and positive results.

Albert Einstein had faith and removed all limitations from his mind and, as a result, he was able to reveal mathematical and scientific principles that the rest of the world did not know existed. Professor Einstein had a mind full of faith that allowed him to make these discoveries. If instead his mind had been filled with fear, doubt, apprehension about criticism from the academic world, or other negative thoughts, these wonderful discoveries of his would have never been made.

In much the same way, George Washington used his faith to achieve victory over the British at Valley Forge, over an enemy that was far superior in arms and number to his own troops. This strong faith and belief led Washington to obtain freedom for his fellow men and to help create one of the world's greatest nations.

This is not an age favorable to the skeptic or the Doubting Thomas. The person who thinks it cannot be done is kept busy trying to get out of the way of those who are doing it. This is an age when anything can happen, and this is because men have discovered that they can do anything they believe they can.

—NAPOLEON HILL

If your world is filled with limitations, misery, doubt, and want, it is because you have not aroused the positive faculties of your mind. You must realize that your mind is like a laboratory and you have in your possession faith that allows you to create anything you desire.

If the possibilities of the future are judged by the achievements of the past, and I firmly believe they are, then the so-called undiscovered miracles are more numerous than those which we have already seen.

Think of how people like Mahatma Gandhi, Orville and Wilbur Wright, Albert Einstein, Thomas Edison, Henry Ford, Alexander Graham Bell, and countless others were able to achieve miracles and change history because of their faith that removed the negative limitations from their minds. Truly, the importance of faith in our own abilities cannot be overstated.

Faith simply means the visualization of and belief in the attainment of one's desires. Faith is one of the most important principles in the pursuit of wealth, and any other worthwhile achievement.

Think of faith as the chemist of the mind. Faith, love, and sex are among the most powerful of all the positive emotions and when you blend these three emotions, along with a thought or idea, the thought almost instantly reaches the subconscious mind. The blending of ideas and these emotions will cause the subconscious mind to pick up, at once, the vibrations of thought and then will translate the thought into its spiritual equivalent with the aid of Infinite Intelligence. I'm sure you have heard of the phrase, "thoughts are things." This simply means that anything we see in the physical world first began as a thought in someone's mind, and this has been proven to be true over and over again.

It may not always be easy to develop faith, but it is of utmost importance if you ever expect to have financial wealth and the other riches that life offers.

It is important to understand and use the principle of autosuggestion in order to gain the highest benefits of faith. Just like with autosuggestion, faith is a state of mind and can be reached or created by the use of repetition. Constantly repeat or affirm to yourself that you can accomplish anything, and watch how fast your faith grows!

For instance, take the example of acquiring financial wealth. This is a thought impulse that we call a definite major purpose or desire. By using autosuggestion, faith, and repeating your desire to yourself on a regular basis, you can convince your subconscious mind that you believe you will get what you are seeking, and believe me, you will get it.

The repetition or affirmation of orders to your subconscious mind is the only known method of developing faith. You must constantly tell yourself that you can achieve anything, and by doing so, you will be eliminating any limitations that are set up in your mind by fear, worry, or negative thoughts.

When people first come into contact with crime, they abhor it. This is due to the fact that most of us are taught right from wrong as children. However, if people remain in situations where they come in constant contact with crime, they adapt and become accustomed to it. They learn to endure it. If people remain in contact with crime for

Confidence is the basis of all personal achievement. With it, you get whatever you go after, because no one wishes to stand in your way.

—NAPOLEON HILL

a long period of time, they learn to accept this behavior as a natural part of life and no longer see it as wrong, the way they initially did. This fact clearly illustrates how any impulse or thought that is repeated is eventually acted upon by the subconscious mind. The subconscious then transforms the idea into its physical equivalent.

ALL THOUGHTS WHICH HAVE BEEN EMOTIONALIZED AND SPURRED WITH FAITH begin at once to translate themselves into their physical equivalent or counterpart.

Emotions give thoughts vitality and life, and lead to action. The subconscious mind will act upon any impulse that is emotionalized, whether it is negative and destructive or positive and constructive. This explains the phenomenon that most people refer to as "bad luck."

Millions of people believe they are doomed to poverty and failure and see no way out of their condition. They believe they have no control over their situation and don't realize that they are actually creating their bad situation by harboring negative thoughts. The negative thoughts are picked up

Faith! If you know some person who believes in you, who knows all of your faults and still stands by you faithfully on account of the good there is in you, be careful not to lose that person's friendship. With the aid of one such person, you can become strong. With the aid of two such persons, you can become a giant. With the aid of three such persons, you can become a genius and rise to heights of achievement such as most people never dream of attaining.

—Napoleon Hill

by the subconscious mind and are translated into their physical counterparts.

You can achieve your definite major purpose by sending that desire to your subconscious with the belief or faith that you will actually reach your goal. Your belief and faith in yourself, nothing else, determines the action of the subconscious mind. Think about that—it is very important.

Hopefully, you have learned through your own experiences that the benefits of faith combined with direct instructions are outstanding.

If we can become criminals by constantly associating with crime, then we can develop faith by taking the time to constantly repeat to our subconscious that we can achieve anything we truly believe in with a burning desire to attain it.

It is important to develop the state of mind known as faith, but you must also take action on that faith or belief. People often say, "have faith" or "just believe," yet it is not enough to simply believe that something will happen, you must take action and put the plans that have been placed in your mind into effect in order to achieve worthwhile results.

Your world consists largely of what you think. No one on earth can take away from you your right to think as you please; therefore, your destiny is eternally bound up in the nature of your dominating thoughts.

—NAPOLEON HILL

Faith is the eternal magic that gives life, power, and action to our thought impulses.

Faith is the starting point of the accumulation of all riches.

Faith is the only known antidote for failure.

Faith is the basis of all so-called miracles and all events or mysteries that cannot be explained by science.

Faith is the element that, when combined with prayer, gives a person direct communication with Infinite Intelligence.

Faith is the element which transforms the ordinary vibration of thought, repeated by the infinite mind of man, into its spiritual equivalent.

Each of us believes what is repeated to our subconscious mind, whether true or false. This is true for the letters of the alphabet, multiplication tables, or the idea that we can accomplish anything we desire. However, we also tend to believe our own limitations, such as that some task is impossible, or we don't have the necessary skills to accomplish it.

The life we are living today is a result of the thoughts we held in our minds yesterday. It is fortunate that our environment can be molded into whatever we desire simply by utilizing the mental assets we all possess. In the same way, our environment can be shaped into a world of despair, depravity, and fear by utilizing negative emotions and mental liabilities. Often, our greatest handicap is our lack of self-confidence, but this can be overcome by the use of autosuggestion.

In order to properly develop self-confidence, it is important to develop positive affirmations to tell yourself, over and over again. An example of such an affirmation is given below:

"I know I have the ability to achieve my definite major purpose in life; therefore I demand of myself persistent, continuous action toward its attainment.

I realize the dominating thoughts of my mind will eventually reproduce themselves into physical reality; therefore I will concentrate my efforts on thinking about the person I intend to become, thus creating in my mind a clear, mental picture of that person.

Through the principle known as autosuggestion, I know any desire I hold in my mind will eventually express itself in its physical form and that my subconscious mind will provide the plans for achieving my goal.

I have written down a description of my definite chief aim, in a clear manner, and I will persist with faith and a positive mental attitude until I've developed the self-confidence necessary for the attainment of that which I desire.

I realize that no wealth or position of responsibility can long endure unless built upon truth and justice. I will not engage in any transaction that does not benefit all whom it affects. I will succeed by attracting the forces I wish to use and the cooperation of other people. Others will cooperate with me because I will cooperate with others. I will cause others to believe in me because I believe in myself. I know that a negative attitude toward others will never bring me success.

I will sign my name to this formula of self-confidence and read it aloud at least once a day with faith that it will influence my thoughts and actions so that I will become a self-reliant and successful person."

Autosuggestion is important and has been proven to lead to success for those who understand

No man has a chance to enjoy permanent success until he begins to look in the mirror for the real causes of all his mistakes.

—Napoleon Hill

and apply it. On the other hand, autosuggestion can be used in a destructive manner. Negative application of the principle will reap a life of misery and poverty.

The subconscious mind does not make a distinction between negative or positive thoughts. It translates what thought impulse is given to it into a physical equivalent. The subconscious mind will translate into reality a thought driven by fear just as quickly as it will translate into reality a thought driven by courage and faith.

Just as electricity can provide many benefits if used appropriately, or wreak havoc and destroy lives if mishandled, so can the use of the autosuggestion principle. The choice is yours whether you want to live a life of riches, or a life of poverty.

The law of autosuggestion, through which any person may rise to high altitudes of achievement which stagger the imagination, is best described in the following poem, "The Man Who Thinks He Can":

If you think you are beaten,
　　you are

If you think you dare not, you
    don't

If you like to win, but you
       think you can't

It is almost certain you won't.

If you think you'll lose, you've
    lost

For out of the world we find,

Success begins with a
     fellow's will

It's all in the state of mind.

If you think you are outclassed,
     you are

You've got to think high to rise,

You've got to be sure of your-
    self before

You can ever win a prize.

Life's battles don't always go

To the stronger or faster man,

But soon or late the man who
    wins,

Is the man who thinks he can.

WALTER D. WINTLE

Faith is composed of three elements, namely, belief, confidence, and action. If you reread the above poem and concentrate closely on the words, you will realize that within you lies a sleeping seed of achievement. You only have to awaken this seed, and act to aid its growth, in order to reach heights which you previously never dreamed of.

Faith is the keystone to the arch of your temple of success. Without it, your building will tumble.

—NAPOLEON HILL

Who told you it couldn't be done? What great achievement has he to his credit that entitles him to use the word "impossible" so freely?

—Napoleon Hill

The man who receives no pay from his labor except that which comes in his pay envelope is underpaid and cheated, no matter what his salary may be. The real pay for labor comes from the joy one gets out of performing it. The money one receives is merely incidental.

—NAPOLEON HILL

A Definite Chief Aim will teach you how to save wasted effort and to fix your heart and hand upon a definite, well-conceived purpose in life.

—NAPOLEON HILL

SELF-DISCIPLINE

There is no single requirement for success as important as self-discipline. It means taking possession of your mind. There are priceless benefits you will receive when you master this principle and here are some of them.

- First, your imagination will become more alert.
- Your enthusiasm will become keener.
- Your initiative will become more active.
- Your self-reliance will be greater.
- The scope of your vision will be widened.
- You will look at the world through different eyes.
- Your personality will become more magnetic.

- Your hopes and ambitions will be stronger.
- Your faith will be more powerful.

The emotions are states of mind and therefore subject to your control and direction. You will be able to exercise the seven positive emotions; namely:

- Love
- Sex
- Hope
- Faith
- Enthusiasm
- Loyalty
- And Desire

And you'll be able to eliminate the seven negative emotions, which are:

- Fear
- Jealousy
- Hatred
- Revenge
- Greed

- Anger
- And Superstition

You will recognize that emotional control is of increased importance to you when you realize that most people allow emotions to rule their lives, and that these emotions largely rule the world. Habits are automatic acts which you perform daily, either for good or for bad. Self-discipline is a matter of adopting constructive habits. What you really are, what you really do, either your failures or your successes, are the result of your habits. Isn't it a blessing then that these habits can be self-made and that the most important habits are those of thought?

You will display in your deeds the nature of your thought habits, and when you have gained control over your thought habits, you will have gone a long way toward the mastery of self-discipline. Definite motives are the beginning of thought habits. Self-discipline without definiteness of motive is impossible and, besides, it would be worthless to you, for it would have nothing to act upon. No one ever does anything without a motive.

It has been said that emotion without reason is

man's greatest enemy. Anyone who wishes to succeed must use reason and emotions with a balance of each. Hardly a day passes in anyone's life without his feeling like doing something his reason tells him he shouldn't do.

Both the head reasoning and the heart emotions need a master and they will find such a master in the faculty of the willpower. The ego acting through the will acts as a presiding judge, but only for the person who has deliberately trained his ego for the job through self-discipline. In the absence of this self-discipline, the ego minds its own business and lets the reason and the emotions fight their battles as they please and, in this case, the man within whose mind the fight is carried on often gets badly hurt.

It is because of this inward conflict which goes on without a presiding judge or referee that so many people have problems which they are unable to solve for themselves, which leads to them running to the psychiatrist. This conflict is one of the basic causes of the increase of neuroses in our culture today. In other words, the need for self-discipline is increasing as our culture becomes

Occasions of defeat are permanent only in the mind that accepts them as such.

—NAPOLEON HILL

more complicated and increases its demands upon our minds.

There are four items which we must exert strong self-discipline over at all times, namely:

- Our appetite, that is, for food and drink
- Our mental attitude
- The use of our time, and
- Definiteness of purpose

And each of these requires a great deal of self-discipline. In the case of the first, food and drink, it's a well-established fact that many people don't exercise enough discipline in regard to the amount and the kinds of food they put into their body. After a certain point has been reached in which the actual needed nourishment is supplied to restore body tissues worn out by our physical and mental effort, additional food only imposes an extra strain upon the organs and accumulates a surplus which builds fat tissues. Too much fat, especially in middle and later age, tends to reduce one's efficiency and to shorten one's life.

The same thing holds true with drinking alcoholic beverages. There is a necessity for controlling your desire for strong drinks, otherwise you're inviting disaster and failure.

One's mental attitude in regard to everything is extremely important because all through life a positive mental attitude is the only frame of mind in which you can express definiteness of purpose or by which you can induce anyone else to cooperate with you. I think it's very important to remind you that the Creator has given you the right of control over but one thing in all this world and that's your mental attitude. You can use it negatively to attract all the things you don't want, or by neglecting it you will allow the weeds to take over the garden spot of your mind, or you can pay the price to learn the ways of keeping it positive and to attract things you do want in life.

This means as well that our ability to get along with others, which is one of the most important characteristics in the lives of all of us, is determined mainly by our frame of mind or our positive mental attitude.

The third item on the list is time, and it may surprise you to know that most of us don't realize that how we spend our time is extremely important. There is an old saying that wasting time is sinful, and it's sad, but true. I can't tell you how to spend your time, but I can point out to you that your time is the most precious asset you have. It's like money in the bank if it's used correctly, and like money in the bank, it should be spent under strict self-discipline and not wasted.

Time is funny stuff, you can't save it except by spending it wisely. The average person works eight hours a day. He needs approximately eight hours for sleep and this leaves another eight hours for free time to invest as he pleases.

It is the way in which this free time is used that makes the difference between success and failure in life. Think this over and make up your mind that you are going to set up a chart for the expenditure of your allotment of 24 hours.

Budgeting of time is very important. It makes one aware of the amount of time one wastes when it's not budgeted. And it's also interesting to know that the fourth item, namely definitiveness of purpose, fits right in with this use of time.

Unless one has a definite goal and a means of

attaining it, the problem of what to do will always arise in one's mind, and it's interesting to know that analyzing your capabilities and then writing down your aims and plans requires a great deal of time, thought, and energy, and the disciplining of your ideas to get what you want out of life. And it's important to realize that even Infinite Intelligence, as all powerful as it is, can't help you if you don't make up your mind what it is that you want and where you are going.

Here is a story that illustrates the point perfectly. We see a man start out with a basket, just a 25-cent basket and a handful of bananas. That is all he has, except for a major purpose to become a successful businessman. He starts peddling his bananas and if he sells one, he can eat one during the day. If he doesn't sell one, he can't afford to eat one. By and by he makes enough to buy a little pushcart. On the cart he has oranges, grapes, and pears in addition to bananas. Well, the first thing you know, he has a little hole-in-the-wall store in a shack somewhere near a parking lot, perhaps. Next, he leases the lot and builds a building on it and before you know it, he buys the lot outright and puts up a modern store in which he does a thriving business. And the next thing we know, he is the founder of the Bank of Italy in a saloon in San Francisco, later to become the head of the largest chain of banks in the world, the great Bank of America chain, and his name is Amadeo Pietro Giannini. All this really happened and was possible because this poor peddler had definiteness of purpose, the persistence, the faith, and the self-discipline to make what he had fit his goals.

You and I started from a slightly improved economic level than Mr. Giannini and we have the benefit of this Success Philosophy, but we, too, must pay the price tag on success.

In order to be successful, we must pay the price. One can't get something for nothing. If one does, it's not appreciated nearly as much as when he worked for it. There were times in my own experience when I didn't have a friend, not even among my relatives, except my stepmother. And sometimes I wondered if she wasn't putting on an act just to encourage me.

There were times when my opponents said, well, he's talking about success and he doesn't have two nickels of his own to rub together. And the worst part of it was, they were right.

I put in some 20 years of extreme self-discipline. I had to discipline myself to put up with the widespread lack of interest in this philosophy. I had to have sufficient self-interest and self-discipline to carry me through those lean years.

No matter who you are, when you first start out, you will encounter seemingly insurmountable obstacles. I well remember the first class to whom I taught this philosophy. It consisted of six people and four of them walked out on me before the class was over. One of them refused to pay because he said he didn't feel that he had received his money's worth. And confidentially, I think he told the truth.

You have to have self-discipline to get over those rough spots in the beginning. You have to discipline your tastes and your standard of living and make them fit what you have right now, until the time comes when you can have more.

The best way to avoid such discouragement is to confide in no one but those who have a genuine sympathy with your cause and an understanding of your possibilities; otherwise, keep your plans to yourself and let your actions speak. Adopt the motto, "Deeds not words." It was Thomas Edison's motto and if it was good enough for this great man of vision, it's a good motto for all of us.

In my younger days, I used to go around, not only with a chip on my shoulder but a whole block of wood and a sign up there that said I just dare you to knock this off. And somebody did always come along and knock it off, too. As I acquired self-discipline, I took down that sign. That helped some, but not enough. I found I had to reduce the block to a chip, which helped some more. But finally, I said to myself, I will have a shoulder that is fully free with no chip for anyone to knock off. Well, I stopped expecting people to find fault and, lo and behold, the world around me began to change from one of disharmony to one of harmony and coopera- tion. I changed the world I lived in simply by chang- ing my own mental attitude.

At one time I didn't like people who wore loud, flashy clothes. And do you know what I did to work on that? I started wearing them myself, just to see how these people would feel. In other words, by getting the other fellow's viewpoint, I found that under the same circumstances my reaction was much the same as his. When you get into that positive frame of mind and quit disliking people just because they are different from you, you will find this a more friendly world in which to live. If you want to get people to see your way or to co-operate with you, do your part by first getting into the right frame of mind to attract them. You'll be astonished at how quickly they will change their attitude toward you.

Self-discipline then is the procedure by which one coordinates the mind or, more clearly stated, the six departments of the mind. These departments of the mind, which are subject to control by the individual, are:

1. The ego—this is the seat of the willpower and acts as a Supreme Court with the power to reverse, modify, change, or eliminate altogether the entire work of all the other departments of the mind.

2. The faculty of the emotions—here is generated the driving force which sets one's thoughts, plans, and purposes into action.

3. The faculty of reason—this is where one may weigh, estimate, and properly evaluate the products of the imagination and of the emotions.

4. The faculty of the imagination—this is where one may create ideas, plans, and methods of attaining desired ends.

5. The conscience—this is where one may test the moral justice of one's thoughts, plans, and purposes.

6. The memory—this serves as the keeper of records of all experiences and as a filing cabinet for all sense perceptions and the inspiration of Infinite Intelligence.

When these departments of the mind are coordinated and properly guided by self-discipline, they enable a person to negotiate his way through life with a minimum of opposition from other people.

The ego, which is the seat of your real power, must remain strong. I'll explain it in reference to myself, but you can do the same with your own ego. I will describe the three imaginary walls of outer defense I keep around the ego, which I know as Napoleon Hill. Starting with the outside one and working in, the first wall is just high enough to keep away from me the people who really have no business getting to me to take up my time. However, this outer wall has several doors in it and it's not too difficult to enter one of them. If a person can establish a reasonable right to my time, I open one of the doors and let him in; but he has to establish that right.

The next wall is very much taller and there is only one door in it, which I watch very closely. The number of persons who get in through that door is comparatively smaller. Before the door swings open to admit anyone, he must have established the fact that he has something which I want or that we have something in common and which will be mutually helpful.

The third and final wall is so tall that no person in the world except my Creator has ever scaled it and there are no doors in it, whatsoever. Not even my own wife is ever allowed inside that wall because it surrounds and protects the ego of Napoleon Hill. Let me tell you, that if you are going to open the door of your ego and personality and let anyone who chooses walk in and out and influence your life, they will take away a lot of things that you won't want them to have and also leave some you shouldn't have. I admonish you to throw a protective wall around your own mind and have a place where you can retire to yourself, where you can commune with Infinite Intelligence undisturbed.

Reason isn't the only factor over which we must exercise control, however. We must exercise control over the so-called second division of the mind, the faculty of emotions. This is very important because of the necessity for balancing the emotions or feelings of the heart with the faculty of reason or the judgment of the head, so that whenever a problem is encountered and one makes an approach to solving it by balancing these two, it makes a satisfactory solution possible.

There is another aspect of the emotions which we should consider, because it concerns problems which arise in one's mind in connection with disappointments and failures and the broken hearts that occur as the result of the loss of material things or the loss of friends or loved ones.

Self-discipline is the only real solution for those problems. It begins with the recognition of the fact that there are only two kinds of problems, those

Webster was twenty-two years in writing his dictionary, and Edison was defeated 10,000 times before he completed the incandescent electric lightbulb. Verily, there is virtue in persistence.

—NAPOLEON HILL

you can solve and those you can't solve. The problems which you can solve should be immediately cleared up by the most practical means available, and those which have no solution should be put out of your mind and forgotten.

Self-discipline, which means the mastery over all of your emotions, can close the door between yourself and all unpleasing experiences of the past. You must close the door tightly and lock it securely, so there is no possibility of its being opened again.

Those who lack self-discipline often stand in the doorway and look wistfully back into the past instead of closing the door and looking forward into the future. There can be no compromise with this door-closing business. You must place the power of your will against the door that shuts out the things you wish to forget, or you won't acquire self-discipline.

Self-discipline closes the door tightly against all manner of fears and opens widely the door to hope and faith. It closes the door tightly against jealousy and opens widely a new door to love. Self-discipline looks forward, not backward. It blocks out discouragement and worry. It encourages the positive

Revenge is a form of "black plague" which drives away the sort of thoughts which lead to a worthy achievement, kills off constructive ambition, destroys enthusiasm, dwarfs the imaginative faculty of the brain, undermines self-control, and stands as a barrier to permanent success in a hundred other ways. Revenge is a cuttleworm, which bores from within and destroys the finer emotions of the heart.

—NAPOLEON HILL

emotions and it keeps out the negative emotions. It is developed for the purpose of making your mind strong. It enables you to take possession of your own mind and experience the God-made right to control your own mental attitude. You don't have real self-discipline until you can organize your mind and keep it clear of all disturbing influences.

I would like to give you my creed for self-discipline. The title is Willpower and here it is:

"Recognizing that the power of will is a Supreme Court over all other departments of my mind, I will exercise it daily when I need the urge to action for any purpose; and I will form habits designed to bring the power of my will into action at least once daily.

Emotions: realizing that my emotions are both positive and negative, I will form daily habits which will encourage the development of the positive emotions and aid me in converting the negative emotions into some form of useful action.

Reason: recognizing that both my positive emotions and my negative emotions may be dangerous if they're not controlled and guided to desirable ends, I will be guided by my reason in giving expression to these.

Imagination: recognizing the need for sound plans and ideas for the attainment of my desires, I will develop my imagination by calling upon it daily for help in the formation of my plans.

Conscience: recognizing that my emotions often err in their overenthusiasm and my faculty of reason often is without the warmth of feeling that is necessary to enable me to combine justice with mercy in my judgments, I will encourage my conscience to guide me as to what is right and what is wrong, and I will never set aside the verdicts it renders, no matter what may be the costs of carrying them out.

Memory: recognizing the value of an alert memory, I will encourage mine to become alert by taking care to impress it clearly with all thoughts I wish to recall and by associating those thoughts with related subjects, which I may call to mind frequently.

Subconscious mind: recognizing the influence of my subconscious mind over my willpower,

I will take care to submit to it a clear and a definite picture of my goal in life and all minor purposes leading to my goal. And I shall keep this picture constantly before my subconscious mind by repeating it daily."

The conscience is the faculty which decides upon the moral quality of your actions and motives. If your conscience is always consulted and the counsel is always obeyed, it's a valuable companion and guide. If it is neglected or ignored and insulted by a violation of its advice, it will become an offender and a conspirator who will back you up in your wrongdoing. When this occurs, it is time to take heed because society has had to build a lot of special rooms for people who have let that happen, and the view from these rooms is always obstructed by bars.

A man may deny his conscience momentarily, but the day will come when his conscience, which has been denied or subdued, will turn with fury and torment him all through the days of his life and also during his sleeping at night.

Every person has a little corner in his soul into which he doesn't wish anyone to look. That's why we can deceive ourselves and perhaps why our neighbors know us much better than we do. That short phrase "Let your conscience be your guide" is of great importance, because if your reason says yes and your conscience says no, you had better follow your conscience.

Self-discipline is one of the most important Science of Success principles, perhaps the most important, because, without it, the other principles simply cannot operate. It is the master key to success and wealth, in whatever form you seek it.

AFTERWORD

The Trustees of the Napoleon Hill Foundation hope you have enjoyed and benefited from success. The material was all written by Napoleon Hill (and edited for clarity and brevity by the Foundation). Much of it has not been published for many years, and the rest of it has never been published until now. The unpublished works came from the Foundation's archives

Napoleon's greatest work, *Think and Grow Rich,* was written in the Great Depression and focused, understandably, on success of the monetary kind. His later works placed more emphasis on other types of success, such as the wealth one receives from helping others or living a harmonious family life. The writings we selected were intended to provide guideposts on the road to obtaining success of all kinds. The success principles explained in this book included having a definite purpose, persevering, focusing one's attention, budgeting time, working with others, applying faith in yourself and your objectives, having a positive mental attitude, and maintaining self-discipline. These writings provide a microcosm of the essential principles Napoleon discovered and developed over a lifetime of research, principles you can use to attain the success you desire.

DON GREEN
EXECUTIVE DIRECTOR
NAPOLEON HILL FOUNDATION